# REVIVING GREATER RUSSIA?

*The Future of Russia's Borders with Belarus, Georgia, Kazakhstan, Moldova and Ukraine*

**Herman Pirchner, Jr.**

**American Foreign Policy Council**
Washington, D.C.

**University Press of America,® Inc.**
Lanham · Boulder · New York · Toronto · Oxford

The American Foreign Policy Council is a private educational foundation established in 1982 to bring information to those who make or influence
the policy of the United States, and to assist leaders in the former USSR and
other parts of the world in building democracies and market economies.

The American Foreign Policy Council is incorporated in the District of
Columbia, and is a tax-exempt organization under section 501(c)(3) of the
United States Internal Revenue Code.

American Foreign Policy Council
1521 16th Street, NW
Washington, DC 20036

Printed in the United States of America

University Press of America, ® Inc.
4501 Forbes Boulevard
Suite 200
Lanham, Maryland 20706
UPA Acquisitions Department (301) 459-3366

PO Box 317
Oxford
OX2 9RU, UK

British Library Cataloging in Publication Information Available

Copublished by arrangement with the American Foreign Policy Council.

Library of Congress Control Number: 2005922541
ISBN 0-7618-3200-9 (paperback : alk. ppr.)
ISBN: 978-0-7618-3200-3

TM The paper used in this publication meets the minimum requirements
of American National Standard for Information Sciences - Permanence of
Paper for Printed Library Materials,
ANSI Z39.48 -- 1992

# Table of Contents

# Foreword

More than a decade after the collapse of the Soviet Union, uncertainty about the permanence of Russia's borders with many of the former republics of the USSR continues to underlie tensions between the Kremlin and its neighbors. The potential for expansion, whether peaceful or otherwise, still shapes both Russian foreign and domestic policy.

In *Reviving Greater Russia?*, Herman Pirchner, Jr. has compiled an authoritative assessment of neo-imperialist forces in Russia and their chances of success in Belarus, Georgia, Kazakhstan, Moldova and Ukraine. His extensive travel and meticulous research, made possible through the support of the Smith-Richardson Foundation, have yielded a unique, first-hand look at the ethnic ties, religious frictions and historical bonds that continue to influence politics along Russia's borders.

It is obligatory reading for all those who seek to understand Russia's policies in its "near abroad."


William Schneider, Jr.
Former Undersecretary of State
Board of Advisors, American Foreign Policy Council

# Acknowledgments

This work is the result of a year of research and collaboration by a number of people whose time and dedication are deeply appreciated.

My gratitude to the Smith-Richardson Foundation, whose support made this project possible.

Special thanks go to my wife, Elizabeth Wood, for her patience and support, and for her sharp eye throughout the editorial process. Much-deserved thanks are also due to AFPC Program Officer Annie Earley; AFPC's Vice President for Policy, Ilan Berman; and AFPC Program Associate Artem Agoulnik. Without their assistance and encouragement, this project would not have reached fruition.

Additionally, I would like to thank Mr. Harold Leich, Russian Area Specialist at the European Division of the Library of Congress, Library of Congress Senior Legal Specialist Dr. Peter Roudik, and Dr. Vitaly Shelest. Their expertise and advice were invaluable to drafting the historical sections of *Reviving Greater Russia?*

All of these individuals deserve praise for the outcome of this work. As for any errors contained herein, they are mine alone.

Herman Pirchner, Jr.
Washington, DC
April 2004

# Introduction

How quickly the political map of the world can change. Only 55 sovereign states existed in 1900. One hundred years later, the thirteen empires that dominated world politics in the 20th Century had collapsed, leaving 192 sovereign states in their wake.[1]

These empires ended for many reasons. Following their defeat in World War I, the Ottoman and Austro-Hungarian empires were dismantled by victorious powers. Anti-colonial activism was first among several factors that caused the British and French to withdraw from their colonies. The Soviet Union disintegrated in 1991 simply because Moscow no longer had the will to maintain it. Standing alone against this trend is the Chinese Empire, which, under communist rule in the last half of the 20th Century, regained lost territory.

Regardless of the reason for their failure, the disintegration of empires begot new states whose borders created and continue to exacerbate ethnic tensions, and left substantial economic ties that need to be protected. The former imperial powers have responded to these problems in four basic ways:

### The use of force to regain lost territory

The post-World War I Treaty of Trianon (1920) deprived Hungary of "two-thirds of her territory ... (and) one-third of her Hungarian-speaking (population)."[2] Between 1938 and 1941, Hungary, supported by Germany and Italy, used diplomacy and limited military force to regain lost territory from Czechoslovakia (southern Slovakia and Subcarpathian Rus), Romania (northern Transylvania) and Yugoslavia (Backa).[3] However, these gains were short-lived; having again picked the losing side, Hungary's borders shrank anew in the aftermath of World War II.

Between 1949 and 1951, the People's Republic of China forcefully reimposed control over Tibet, which had declared independence in 1913.

### The use of force to protect or change the leadership of former colonies

The primary practitioner of this strategy has been France, which has "intervened militarily, either to change regimes in sub-Saharan Africa or to restore deposed strongmen, no less than thirty-seven times since 1960."[4]

### The use of diplomacy to regain lost territory

In the aftermath of World War I, Italy, as a member of the victorious Triple Entente, was given the ethnically Slovenian province of Trst, which was renamed Trieste. Following WWII, Trieste was declared a "free territory" under Allied supervision. Through skillful diplomacy, bolstered by its newly acquired NATO membership, Italy largely regained control of Trieste by 1954. Italian sovereignty, however, only became uncontested in 1975, with the signing of an Italian-Yugoslav border agreement.[5]

*The use of diplomacy to maintain influence*

Peaceful relations have been the norm between most successor states to empires and parts of their former territory. This is true not only of territories that the imperial power has no serious interest in re-colonizing or annexing (e.g., British colonies in Africa), but also of areas that the former imperial power might covet but has, for political and/or military reasons, no chance of regaining (such as South Tyrol, a former Austrian province placed under Italian sovereignty in the aftermath of World War I).

As the successor state to a collapsed empire, the Russian Federation cannot and will not ignore parts of its former empire. One or more of the above policies will be implemented by the Russian Federation – perhaps different policies for different parts of the former USSR.

# The Empire Question in Russian Policy

In the last days of 2001, with little fanfare or public opposition, a remarkable new Russian law went into effect.[6] Entitled "On Admission to the Russian Federation and the Formation Within the Russian Federation of a New Subject," it makes clear that "a foreign state, or a part thereof, may be accepted into the Russian Federation as a new federal entity."[7] The law further specifies that the proposal to join Russia "…must originate from a given foreign state."[8] A formal treaty between the foreign state and Russia would then outline the procedure by which the foreign state, or a part of it, would be incorporated into the Russian Federation.

Enacted by President Vladimir Putin and key parliamentary supporters, this legislation is no less than a blueprint for enlarging the Russian Federation - one now being given new attention by the Kremlin. Thus, in his March 2004 address to the Russian State Duma, newly-selected Prime Minister Mikhail Fradkov confirmed that, "in light of economic growth and questions of demography," the Russian government would "in the future simplify grants of citizenship to Russians living abroad."[9] When paired with the draft national security concept authored by Defense Minister Sergei Ivanov in late 2003, which authorizes the use of force to protect Russian citizens living beyond the borders of Russia - not to mention the gathering momentum of a Moscow-dominated "Single Economic Space" harmonizing the economies of Russia, Belarus, Kazakhstan and Ukraine - such comments are mounting evidence that the Kremlin is actively contemplating the creation of a "Greater Russia."

Such an idea is not new. In March 1994, Alexander Solzhenitsyn was among the first to publicly proclaim the ideological justification for such action:

The trouble is not that the USSR broke up – that was inevitable. The real trouble, and a tangle for a long time to come, is that the breakup occurred mechanically along false Leninist borders, usurping from us entire Russian provinces. In several days we lost 25 million ethnic Russians – 18 percent of our entire nation....[10]

Russia has truly fallen into a torn state: 25 million have found themselves 'abroad' without moving anywhere, by staying on the lands of their fathers and grandfathers. Twenty-five million – the largest diaspora in the world by far. How dare we turn our back to it? ...The optimal solution is a Union of the three Slavic republics and Kazakhstan.[11]

Mr. Solzhenitsyn repeated the call for Slavic unity on the floor of the Duma, Russia's lower house of parliament, in February 1995. That he was given such a forum to call for expanding the Russian Federation was a sure sign of serious political support for the idea.

More recently, Dmitry Rogozin, a Deputy Chairman of the Russian Duma, has been championing the same concept. In his book *We Will Reclaim Russia for Ourselves*, Rogozin makes the case that:

> The lack of understanding of the Russian question, the division of the Russian nation gives us the feeling of an unrepaid debt. And debts must be repaid.
>
> Russians... should discuss out loud the problem of a divided people that has an historic right to political unification of its own land.
>
> We (Russians) must present ourselves with the problem of a union, no matter how unrealistic this idea is in today's conditions. And we must create conditions to result in the environment with which Germany dealt for forty years coming out united in the end.[12]

Solzhenitsyn and Rogozin are hardly alone. A January 2001 poll found that 61 percent of Russians, 53 percent of Ukrainians, and 69 percent of Belarussians favor unification of their states into one country.[13]

The reason is not hard to fathom. Much of the territory of the former Soviet Union (e.g., Belarus, parts of Georgia, Northern Kazakhstan, Eastern Ukraine, and the Transdneister region of Moldova), separated from the Russian Federation by the USSR's collapse, remains deeply oriented toward Russia. Several of Kazakhstan's northern provinces and a majority of the population in Moldova's Transdneister (now the self-proclaimed Dnestr Republic) are ethnically Slavic. At least 20 percent of Ukrainians are ethnically Russian, with a larger number thought to be descended from both Russian and Ukrainian parentage. Georgia's Abkazian and Ossetian populations would rather be minorities in Russia than minorities in Georgia. Finally, it is widely believed that the Belarussians, not having a strong identity independent of Russia, would vote to join Russia in a free election.

Of course, these sentiments may never lead to the expansion of the Russian Federation. Economic limitations, the difficulty of domestic consensus, and divergent foreign policy priorities all remain political constraints on the concept of a "Greater Russia." But the legal basis for such a move has been laid by Moscow, and its pursuit may be the major goal of Russian President Vladimir Putin's second term.

Pavel Borodin, a longtime Kremlin official and current Putin-appointed head of the fledgling Russia-Belarus Union, believes that "the Russian president could become head of a confederation initially linking Russia with Belarus, but then spreading to other former Soviet countries... After the end of his (Putin's) second term, he needs to have (another) first but very long term ... I think that Mr. Putin agrees."[14]

In any case, the newly independent countries of Belarus, Georgia, Kazakhstan, Moldova and Ukraine will remain a top, if not *the* top, foreign policy priority for the Russian Federation. In its conduct, Moscow's approach will be colored by its historic and evolving relationship with the territory of those countries.

# BELARUS

BELARUS
Area: 207,600 Km Sq.
Population: 10,322,151

Major Cities:
Minsk (1.68 Million) capital
Gomel (0.48 Million)
Vitebsk (0.34 Million)

# BELARUS

## Early History

The territory of Belarus fell under the successive control of Kiev Rus' (beginning in the 9th Century), Lithuania (1240), the confederation of Poland and the Grand Duchy of Lithuania (1385), and then the Polish-Lithuanian Commonwealth (1565).

Russia acquired virtually all the territory of contemporary Belarus through the three partitions of Poland. In 1772, the first partition brought the eastern part of Belarus under Russian rule. Belarus' central part was absorbed through the second partition in 1793. Subsequently, almost all of the remaining territory of present-day Belarus came under Russian sovereignty following the third partition in 1795.[15]

With some exceptions (e.g., the solidarity shown by some in support of the Polish-Lithuanian uprising of January 1863), Russian sovereignty was peacefully accepted by the Belarussian people. Real opposition to Tsarist rule came only with World War I.

Opposition to the war grew with the mounting casualties of German-Russian fighting on Belarussian territory. These anti-war passions melted into the anti-Tsarist movements that culminated in the 1917 February and October revolutions. But the inability of the fledgling Soviet state to effectively prosecute the war resulted in the March 1918 Treaty of Brest-Litovsk, giving most of Belarussian territory to Germany. That same month, the Central Committee of the Belarus Rada (legislature) proclaimed the nullification of the Brest-Litovsk Treaty and the creation of the independent Belarussian Democratic Republic. The new state's independence was to be guaranteed by the German government.

However, the fall of the German government in October 1918 created a power vacuum that permitted Moscow-backed Bolsheviks to take control by force. They established the Belarussian Soviet Socialist Republic (SSR) on January 1, 1919. In its original form, this new state was also to be short-lived, because of the Polish-Soviet War. The defeat of the Trotsky-led Red Army by the troops of Polish General Jozef Pilsudski resulted in the 1921 Treaty of Riga that divided Belarus into three parts. The western part became Poland, the central portion became the reconstituted Belarussian SSR, and the eastern portion became part of the Russian SSR. The territory of the Belarussian SSR was expanded in 1924 and 1926 through the absorption of ethnically Belarussian regions given to Russia through the Treaty of Riga.

Pursuant to the Molotov-Ribbentrop pact, the Soviet Union invaded Poland in September 1939 and held control of the western portion of what is today's Belarus until June 1941, when Germany attacked the Soviet Union. The invading Nazis regained not only western Belarus but other Belarussian territory as well. In the summer of 1944, Soviet troops recaptured this territory and proceeded to establish the current borders of Belarus. This status quo persisted until August 25, 1991, when Belarus declared independence.

## The Russian and Soviet Eras

Throughout the Russian and Soviet eras, efforts were made to "Russify" Belarus. These largely successful attempts centered primarily on the question of language. In today's Belarussian cities, Russian is the language of choice. In the villages, the Belarussian language is used, but it is important to understand that it is not very different from Russian. The large majority of the words, as well as the grammar, is the same. A person speaking only Belarussian and one speaking only Russian have little trouble communicating.

## Independent Belarus: 1991-2003

On August 25, 1991, Belarus' Supreme Soviet (legislature) voted to formalize Belarussian independence. The first post-Soviet Belarussian government, headed by Stanislau Shuskevich, was wary of establishing a union with Russia beyond that of normalized bilateral economic relations. Belarus thus refused to sign the Commonwealth of Independent States (CIS) Collective Security Treaty of 1992 (the Tashkent Treaty), out of fear that it would violate the new government's neutrality. Two years later, however, a preliminary agreement on a Russian-Belarussian monetary union was signed by the Prime Ministers of the two countries.

In the early years of Belarussian independence, the Shuskevich government actively attempted to implement liberal economic and political reforms. But these efforts failed to produce the desired results, and created a domestic backlash against further liberalization on the part of the Belarussian population. In 1994, a collective farm manager, Aleksandr Lukashenko, was overwhelmingly elected President of Belarus in a run-off election, after campaigning on a platform of anti-corruption and Soviet nostalgia. Over the next ten years, Lukashenko steadily consolidated power in his effort to make Belarus a neo-Soviet state, while signing more than a dozen other treaties or agreements with Russia in hopes of unifying the two countries.

These popular documents were sound politics for both sides, because they represented the will of both the Russian and Belarussian people. But, at least from the Belarussian side, there was no serious intent to join Russia. The reason lies, in large part, with Belarussian President Aleksandr Lukashenko's desire to retain power as a sovereign head of state.

By 1996, both the parliament and the court system were no longer effective curbs on Lukashenko's by-then dictatorial powers. The Soviet nature of today's Belarus is immediately evident to visitors, who are often openly followed by state security. Belarussian citizens have another reason to remember the old Soviet Union – Belarus was the first former Soviet Republic to require its citizens to acquire official permission before traveling abroad, and to reintroduce the state emblems of the Soviet era.

## The Future of Belarus

On August 14, 2002, Russian President Vladimir Putin proposed that a spring 2003 referendum on the merger of Belarus and Russia be held in both countries.[16] That vote never occurred, in no small measure because, under Putin's plan, Belarus' six regions would have been added to the 89 regions of the Russian Federation. The plan would have further provided for elections for the President of the newly-created state. For Lukashenko the plan was, of course, unacceptable because it would destroy the sovereignty of Belarus and relegate him to being, at most, one of 95 governors in the expanded Russian Federation. His view is not likely to change, nor is the fact that a referendum on unification would likely pass in both Russia and Belarus.

Partly as a means of dealing with this popular sentiment, Belarus has entered into the newly-created "Single Economic Space" (SES), whose Russian-dominated administrative body is designed to assume part of Belarus' economic sovereignty. But even if the SES works as planned, the way to a full merger is directly connected to the fate of Lukashenko. If he falls from power, Russia may have an easier time working with new leadership. If an alternative and Russia-friendly leadership becomes available, it will have the strong support of Moscow, and Lukashenko's political future will be profoundly threatened. And if an acceptable alternative to Lukashenko does not naturally arise, Moscow policy-makers can be expected to create one, and do so before the end of Vladimir Putin's second term. As discussed on page 4, assuming control of a united Russian-Belarussian state could be an elegant way for Putin to remain in power once his constitutionally-mandated term of office in Russia runs out. Regardless of the reason, Lukashenko will eventually be gone and it is likely that Belarus' merger with the Russian Federation will follow not far behind.

# GEORGIA

GEORGIA
Area: 69,700 Km Sq.
Population: 4,934,413

Major cities:
Tbilisi (1.08 Million) capital
Batumi (0.12 Million)

# GEORGIA

## Early History

Over its more than 2,500 year history, the Georgian state has dominated many smaller ethnic groups native to the Caucasus. But Georgian history is not only that of a small empire; Georgia has often been a small part of other empires as well. Its masters have included Mongols, Arabs, Greeks, Persians, and Russians. Much of its territory was also ruled by the Turks, whose Ottoman government was responsible for the Islamic conversion of the Abkhaz (marginally religious today) and the Ajaris (many of whom still maintain a Muslim identity).

## The Russian and Soviet Eras

Russia gained control of Georgia in stages. Eastern Georgia came under a Russian protectorate in 1783 through the Treaty of Georgievsk. Russian control of the remaining ethnically-Georgian regions was achieved in 1801 – the year Georgian royalty was exiled by order of the Tsar. Full pacification of this region was not immediately achieved, however. Armed forces loyal to the king continued to resist until 1813. This was also the year that Persia's lingering claims to Georgia were renounced under the 1813 Treaty of Gulistan. Other parts of the Georgian Empire were subdued successively, as noted by the official website of the Georgian Parliament:

> At first, Russia took under its protection local political bodies
> (1803 Megrelia Princedom; 1804 Imereti Kingdom; 1810
> Guria and Abkhazia Princedoms; 1833 Svaneti Princedom),
> and then gradually abolished them by the complete annexation
> of their territories (Imereti-1810; Guria-1828; Megrelia-
> 1857; Svaneti-1858; Abkhazia-1864).[17]

Full consolidation of the territory of contemporary Georgia occurred only in 1878, when Russian military success over Ottoman forces led to the annexation of what is now southwest Georgia (Ajaria).

During the chaos of the Russian Civil War, Georgia declared and maintained independence for three years (1918-1921) before losing it again to Moscow. Between 1922 and 1936, Georgia was part of the Soviet Union's Transcaucasian Federation. In 1936, the Transcaucasian Federation was dismantled and the Georgian Soviet Socialist Republic (SSR) became one of the fifteen

Republics of the USSR.

On April 9, 1991, Georgia declared independence from the collapsing Soviet Union.

# Independent Georgia: 1991-2003

Russian-aided Abkhaz fighters drove Georgian troops and civilians out of Abkhazia in 1993. Their success exacerbated the problems Georgian President Eduard Shevardnadze faced in the civil war he was fighting with rebels loyal to former Georgian President Zviad Gamsakhourdia. Finally, Shevardnadze was forced to ask Moscow for assistance, which helped crush the rebel movement.

Shortly thereafter, Georgia reversed its previous position and on October 9, 1993 accepted Moscow's invitation to join the CIS. A Friendship Treaty was also signed with Moscow in 1994, paving the way for Georgian support of Russia in their conflict that year with the breakaway Russian province of Chechnya.

But Georgia's relations with Chechnya were about to change. Discussion of Chechen use of Georgian territory led to a friendly August 1997 meeting between rebel Chechen leader Aslan Maskhadov and Georgian President Eduard Shevardnadze. Simultaneously, relations with Russia were in serious decline. Some observers even thought war was possible in the aftermath of Russia's 1999 bombing of Georgian villages located near the Chechen border. Although this act was officially described as a mistake, Moscow's message regarding Georgian/Chechen cooperation was clear.

The Chechen issue again led to heightened tensions in August 2002, when Moscow warned Tblisi to remove armed Chechens from Georgian territory or see them removed by Russian troops. Georgia responded by announcing anti-Chechen military operations in the Pankisi Gorge. Although most Chechens had left the area in advance of the well-publicized Georgian troop movements, thirteen were captured as a result of the maneuvers. After strong and, not surprisingly, contradictory lobbying by both the Russian and Chechen leadership, eight of the thirteen Chechens were given to Moscow and the Chechen's Tblisi office was closed in October 2002.

The above discussion is central to the issue at hand, because the greater the tensions between Russia and Georgia on Chechnya and other issues not related to the territorial integrity of Georgia, the greater incentive Russia will have to back separatists in South Ossetia and Abkhazia. Tbilisi, for its part, feels the need to have additional levers to retain sovereignty over these breakaway territories. Foremost among these is the strong support the international community has articulated for the territorial integrity of Georgia. U.S. Secretary of State Colin Powell was fully in line with the position of the Organization of Security and

Cooperation in Europe (OSCE) when, on December 2, 2003, he warned Russia not to support "breakaway elements seeking to weaken Georgia's territorial integrity."[18] However, such statements alone may not prove to be enough, since they are not likely to result in the removal of Russian troops from Abkhazia and South Ossetia – without which the full exercise of Georgian sovereignty is impossible. This is well understood by all of the parties.

Even before his January 25, 2004 inaugural, Georgian President-elect Mikhail Saakashvili began his campaign for the removal of Russian bases from the territory of Georgia. The breakaway republics, of course, were urging Russian troops to stay. Meanwhile, Deputy Assistant Secretary of State Lynn Pasco was proclaiming that: "We believe deeply in the agreement of all countries of the OSCE…that they will not keep military forces, bases in an area where they are not welcome."[19] A Russian Foreign Ministry spokesman, meanwhile, asserted that Russia had never promised to withdraw the bases.[20]

With the forced resignation of Georgian President Eduard Shevardnadze on November 23, 2003, Georgia's relations with its three autonomous regions have approached a critical juncture. On November 25, 2003 *Nezavisimaya Gazeta* reported that experts "fear that regions of Georgia – Adjaria (Ajaria), South Ossetia and Abkhazia – may break away to declare their sovereignty. Any attempt by Tblisi to send in the army to restore the status quo would surely lead to civil war."[21]

Fighting may become an option in Ajaria if the troops loyal to Ajarian leader Aslan Abashidze choose to resist the efforts of Georgian President Mikhail Saakashvili to reassert Tbilisi's control over this traditionally independent – but ethnically Georgian – region.[22] More likely, Abashidze will stall for time and make some accommodations in hopes that Georgian internal problems will soon lessen President Saakashvili's popularity and, therefore, his capacity to bring Ajaria to heel.[23]

A Tblisi-initiated civil war in Abkhazia or South Ossetia is even more unlikely, since the presence of Russian troops and the history of earlier confrontations argue strongly that Tbilisi would be defeated in renewed fighting. But if war is not a viable option for Tblisi, what is to follow? The key lies in the breakaway regions.

## Abkhazia During the Russian and Soviet Eras

The Abkhaz people never fully accepted their loss of independence. Armed Abkhaz uprisings against Tsarist Russia occurred in 1821, 1824, 1840-2, 1866, and 1877. These recurring rebellions ended only with the forced exile of hundreds of thousands of Abkhazians to Turkey in the aftermath of the fighting in 1866 and 1877. Between 1924 and 1931, Abkhazia existed as a Republic under the Soviet structure before being reduced to an autonomous SSR within the Georgian SSR. From the mid-1940s to the mid-1970s, efforts were made to "Georgianize" Abkhazia. These included promoting the immigration of ethnic Georgians to Abkhazia and the imposition of the Georgian alphabet and language.

Nonetheless, Abkhaz calls for secession from the Georgian SSR were publicly staged in 1957, 1967, and 1978. By 1989, the ethnic Abkhaz population, once a majority, had been diluted to a mere 18 percent of the republic's population. The remainder was comprised of 46 percent ethnic Georgians, 16 percent ethnic Russians, and 20 percent of other nationalities. Still, the ethnic Abkhaz were given a disproportionate number of positions and privileges, thus creating resentment among the non-Abkhaz population.

## Post-Soviet History of Abkhazia

Tensions between the ethnically Georgian residents of Abkhazia and the region's ethnically Abkhaz residents reached the boiling point in 1992. In July of that year, the Abkhazian Parliament voted to reinstate their 1925 Constitution – a document last in effect when Abkhazia was independent of Georgia. In August, the Georgian government further destabilized the situation by sending the Georgian National Guard to Sukhumi, the Abkhazian capital. Hundreds were killed in the ensuing fighting. The Abkhaz leadership, which had fled the capital, pleaded for Russia to intervene.

The tide of battle was tipped by the resulting influx of Russian aircraft and Russian citizen-volunteers (Cossacks, as well as ethnic Kabardins, Cherkess' and Chechens) who fought with the Abkhaz forces. In the end, an estimated 10,000 lives were lost. By September 1993, the remaining Georgian forces were driven out of Abkhazia. Ethnically Georgian civilians followed in large numbers. Nickoloz Vashakidge, Deputy Director of Georgia's National Security Council, asserts that only a few thousand now remain of the ethnic Georgian population that numbered as many as 380,000 in 1989.[24] Eleven years after the fighting, these Georgian refugees from Abkhazia remain an obvious presence, and, therefore, a political issue, in Tblisi. Their hopes of return fade a bit more each year, as their Abkhaz homes have already been given to those who fought with the Abkhaz side.

On August 24, 1993, United Nations Security Council Resolution 858, and subsequent resolutions, provided the basis for an international detachment of 117 unarmed military personnel and 380 civilians to monitor the ceasefire reached on July 27, 1993.[25] By July 1994, however, it was clear that the UN presence was insufficient to establish order. The resulting enactment of Security Council Resolution 937 provided for a deployment of CIS troops to Abkhazia. This CIS peacekeeping force, comprised solely of 3,000 Russian troops,[26] began to patrol a twenty-five-kilometer zone on both sides of the Georgian and Abkhaz border. Excluded from that zone is the Kodori Valley, where no CIS troops are allowed.

At the beginning of 2003, most Abkhazians still held Soviet passports, albeit ones that had been extended several times. Facing an expiration of these passports, and the resulting inability to travel, most Abkhazians chose to accept the Russian citizenship offered to them by Moscow. Agreements reached at the March 2003 meeting of Shevardnadze, Putin, and Abkhazian Prime Minister Gennady Gagulia led to the resolution of some common problems. These included the decision to:

1) return refugees to the Gali region of Abkhazia, where in 1991 over 90 percent of the population had been ethnically Georgian;
2) open the railway between Sochi and Tblisi, and;
3) reopen the Inguri Hydroelectric Power Station in Gali. Electricity from this station would power Abkhazia, as well as parts of Russia and Georgia proper.

This step toward normalcy does not, however, indicate progress in the fundamental problem of sovereignty over Abkhazia. The leverage exerted by Moscow on its former satellite continues to play a decisive role in the stalemate. As former National Security Advisor Zbigniew Brzezinski noted already a decade ago:

> The use of military and economic means to obtain subordination to Moscow has been strikingly evident... [Georgia has learned] that Russia as umpire is not very different from Russia as empire.[27]

# The Future of Abkhazia

The negotiations begun in 1993[28] show no progress on the key issue of Abkhaz sovereignty, and are unlikely to do so in the future. The Abkhazians want independence from Georgia. The Georgians will not accept any reduction in their sovereignty and will not even consider relaxing the blockade or addressing the refugee question until Abkhazia returns to the fold. UN Security Council Resolution 1096, enacted on January 30, 1997, supports Georgia's claims of sovereignty over Abkhazia.[29] Russia, however, shows no signs of cooperation. Quite to the contrary, they have kept open the eventual option of annexing Abkhazia by:

1) granting Russian citizenship to the majority of Abkhazians – a policy decried by Georgian President Shevardnadze in July 2002 as "dis-
guised annexation;"[30]
2) opening, in December 2002, the rail line between Sochi and
Abkhazia, thus economically integrating Abkhazia with Russia; and
3) keeping their military on Abkhaz soil.

If Russia gives the Abkhaz population the option of joining Russia or having Russian troops withdraw (ensuring a war that could return Abkhazia to
Georgian sovereignty), the Abkhaz may choose to be a minority in Russia rather
than a minority in Georgia. Their path would likely be an election (with plenty
of international observers) in which the Abkhaz people would opt for sovereign-
ty. Then, after a period of time, a second vote (in accordance with the new
Russian Federation legislation) would be held to request annexation by Russia.[31]
A possible alternative expounded by Abkhaz Foreign Minister Sergei
Shamba uses the example of America's relationship with the Marshall Islands as
the basis for the new relationship between Russia and Abkhazia.[32]
While one of these options is the most likely outcome, it is not inevitable.
Vakhtang Rcheulishvili, a Deputy Chairman of the Georgian Parliament,
believes that a closer relationship between Tbilisi and Moscow could pave the
way for Moscow to accommodate Georgian interests in Abkhazia.[33] In his view,
the question may ultimately be whether it is better for Russia to have solid
Georgian cooperation on their Muslim problem than to have Abkhazia. Abkhaz
Foreign Minister Shamba, however, was openly dismissive of this idea, telling
the author that "the Georgians have nothing to offer Russia."[34]
Abkhazia, on the other hand, does. Strategically, a deep-water port on the
Black Sea such as the Abkhaz capital of Sokhumi, is important to Russia, partic-
ularly now that its traditional Black Sea port of Sevastopol belongs to Ukraine.
However, the renewed fighting that would inevitably accompany any Russian
withdrawal would have a destabilizing impact on existing Russian territory in the
Caucasus, as well as on Muslim-dominated areas within Russia.
Russian annexation of Abkhazia would be a mixed blessing on other fronts as
well. It would make future expansion of Russian territory an easier sell in
Moscow, but at the same time it would complicate relations with all other countries having potential border problems with Russia. Further, the resulting prece-
dent of secession would be harmful to Russia in places like Chechnya.

# South Ossetia During the Russian and Soviet Eras

Between 1917-21, most Ossetians cooperated with Russia in its confronta-
tion with Georgia. As a result, in 1918, the new Bolshevik government, recog-
nizing the desire of Ossetians to leave Georgian control, created the Ossetian

Autonomous Soviet Socialist Republic. This territory became part of the Mountain Autonomous Republic in 1920, and on June 8, 1920 South Ossetia declared its independence from Georgian control. Georgia sent troops to quell the mutiny. After the deaths of an estimated 5,000 Ossetians, the region was divided in 1922, with the area north of the Greater Mountains becoming the North Ossetian Autonomous Republic within the Soviet Union's Russian, on SSR, and the area south of the Greater Mountains becoming the South Ossetian Autonomous Oblast within the Soviet Union's Georgian SSR.

South Ossetia renewed its efforts to leave Georgia with its 1989 declaration that South Ossetia was part of the Russian SSR, and with its subsequent August 1990 declaration of "sovereignty." The Soviet Republic of Georgia reacted by ending South Ossetia's autonomous status within Georgia in December 1990. The South Ossetian regional legislature responded by taking steps aimed at secession and eventual unification with the North Ossetian Autonomous Republic of Russia. The Georgian government responded by invading South Ossetia. Thousands of casualties resulted.

## Post-Soviet History of South Ossetia

Fighting between the government of the Soviet Republic of Georgia and South Ossetia continued under the government of independent Georgia through-out 1991 and early 1992. During that time, four significant events occurred:

- First, on January 20, 1992, the population of South Ossetia voted in favor of secession from Georgia and integration with Russia's North Ossetia Autonomous Republic within the Russian Federation.
- Second, a population shift took place. Georgia's last pre-inde-pendence census (1989) showed the 98,000 person population of South Ossetia comprised of 67 percent Ossetians, 29 per cent Georgians, and four percent of other nationalities. At the time, more than 60 percent of Georgia's Ossetian population lived outside the boundaries of South Ossetia. Although exact figures are not available, a significant part of this 60 percentis thought to have moved, as a result of the fighting, to either South Ossetia or the Russian Oblast of North Ossetia.[35]
- Third, in April 1992, the Georgian government proclaimed the reestablishment of the South Ossetian Autonomous Oblast. This preceded the July 1992 ceasefire, mediated by then-Russian President Boris Yeltsin, which ended eighteen months of fighting. It was followed by the establishment in 1993 of the Organization for Security and Cooperation in Europe's

(OSCE) 17-person South Ossetia mission.

- Fourth, at a July 5, 2003 news conference in Moscow, Eduard Kokolti, President of the self-proclaimed South Ossetian Republic, who had no contact with the President of Georgia for two years,[37] openly declared that he would see the intent of the 1992 referendum become a reality. To bolster this claim, he noted that over 60 percent of the population of South Ossetia held Russian citizenship and that "if not one hundred percent, than at least ninety-eight percent of the pop ulation of South Ossetia will become Russian citizens in the very near future."[38]

The formal response from the Putin Administration was cautious: "We respect the territorial integrity of Georgia but understand at the same time that the population of South Ossetia is not secure."[39]

As of January 2004, the ongoing talks, begun in 1994, among Georgia, Russia, South Ossetia, and North Ossetia have failed to resolve the situation.

## The Future of South Ossetia

Emerging from a November 27, 2003 meeting with Russian Minister of Foreign Affairs Igor Ivanov, Eduard Kokolti was asked by a journalist, "Does your proposal on South Ossetia integrating into Russia remain valid after your meeting with Ivanov?" Kokolti answered, " It does, indeed, because, I would like to emphasize once again, it is the will of the people of the Republic of South Ossetia. I will follow this and we will continue our attempts to attain the goal. I have to emphasize, however, that we will be doing this by peaceful means only."[40]

This begs the question: what peaceful means are possible? In the most likely scenario, South Ossetia and Abkhazia would jointly declare independence – an independence that would be recognized by Moscow – and, after a period of time, ask to be annexed by the Russian Federation.

The path towards lasting separation from Georgia, however, will be harder for South Ossetia than for Abkhazia. This is because of OSCE pressure on Russia (absent in Abkhazia) and Tbilisi's predisposition to fight harder to keep South Ossetia – in part because approximately 29 percent of the South Ossetian population is ethnically-Georgian. In the words of David Darchiasvilli, President of the Caucasian Institute, "it is (politically) not so acceptable to give South Ossetia independence."[41]

# KAZAKHSTAN

KAZAKHSTAN

<u>Area</u>: 2,717,300 Km Sq.
<u>Population</u>: 16,763,795

<u>Major cities</u>:
Almaty (1.14 Million)
Karaganda (0.44 Million)
Astana (0.31 Million) capital

# KAZAKHSTAN

## Early History

Kazakhstan lies at the heart of the great Eurasian steppe stretching from Mongolia to Hungary. Nomadic tribes roamed this area for more than 1,700 years prior to 1210 CE, when Jenghiz (Gengis) Khan began his conquering sweep out of the Mongolian steppes to the east. All of Kazakhstan, like the rest of Central Asia, became part of the Mongol Empire. After Jenghiz Khan's death, the empire was divided among his sons and their heirs. Northern and western Kazakhstan became part of the Golden Horde territory that extended to Ukraine and Moscow. The bulk of Kazakhstan, along with Transoxiana (today's Uzbekistan) and Western Xinjiang, became part of the Chaghatai Khanate. Late in the 14th century, Timur (Tamerlane) invaded Transoxiana, and occupied part of contemporary Kazakhstan but did not remain.

The Kazakh people did not emerge as a distinct entity until the 15th Century. They are descended from the Mongols and nomadic Turkic tribes. As the Golden Horde disintegrated in the 14th and 15th Centuries, a group of Islamicized Mongols was left in control of northern Kazakhstan. Taking their name from an early 14th Century leader, Ozbeg (Usbek), the Uzbeks spread to the south, mingling with other peoples, eventually crossing the Syr-Darya river to enter Transoxiana, then the decaying empire of Timur's descendants. The two groups split in 1468; those remaining north of the Syr-Darya became the Kazakhs, a Turkic word for free riders, adventurers, or outlaws.

In the late 15th and 16th Centuries, the Kazakh empire stretched across the steppe and deserts, raiding the remnants of the Chaghatai Khanate in the Tian Shan mountains and Xinjiang to the east, as well as the Uzbek Khanate in Transoxiania. In 1563, a Kazakh leader named Kuchum took over the Golden Horde Siberian Khanate, with its capital at Sibir (Tobolsk). Sibir was captured by the Russians in 1582, the first conflict between the Russian and Kazakh peoples. Such conflicts continued into the 17th Century, as the Russians advanced east and south.

During this period of Russian expansion, the Kazakh empire split into three hordes: the Great (or Elder) Horde in the south, the Middle Horde in central and northeast Kazakhstan, and the Little (or Younger) Horde in the west. Each horde was comprised of clans and headed by a khan. These hordes came under severe assault by the Oyrats, a Mongol people who subjugated eastern Kazakhstan, the Tian Shan mountains and parts of Xinjiang to form the Zhungarian empire in the 1630s. This period is remembered in Kazakhstan as the "Great Disaster."

# The Russian and Soviet Eras

The Kazakhs sought Russian support against the Oyrats, and all three Horde Khans swore loyalty to the Russian Tsar between 1731 and 1742. The Russians did not help much against the Oyrats (who were exterminated by the Manchurian Chinese in the 1750s). However, they took the opportunity to create a military presence in Kazakh territories, subsequently bolstered by Russian, Tatar, and Cossack settlers. Russian colonization was met with repeated Kazakh uprisings – the largest being an 1840 uprising led by Middle Horde leader, Kenisary Kasimov (Khan Kene). The khanates were abolished in 1848 although the hordes, as ethnic groups, remained. In 1854, the Russians founded a fort in southeast Kazakhstan called Vrnay, effectively extending Russian control across all of the former Kazakh empire. This fort later became the capital city of Almaty (Alma-Ata).

By some estimates, one-quarter of the Kazakh population (over one million people) died as a result of revolts or famine during the Russian takeover.[42] It became Russian policy to populate the conquered lands. To that end, Kazakhstan became a place of exile and labor camps. Fyodor Dostoevsky and the Ukrainian nationalist writer Taras Shevchenko are among the most famous of those to be forcibly relocated there.

By the 1890s, more than one million Russian peasant settlers had moved to Northern Kazakhstan in the aftermath of the 1861 abolition of serfdom in Russia and Ukraine. This policy was justified by the Vice Chancellor of the Empire, Prince Aleksandr Gorchakov, in his famous 1884 "Circular on Russia's Mission in Central Asia."

> The position of Russia in Central Asia is that of all civilized states which are brought into contact with half-savage nomad populations possessing no fixed social organization. In such cases, the more civilized state is forced in the interest of the security of its frontiers, and its commercial relations, to exercise a certain ascendancy over their turbulent and undesirable neighbors. Raids and acts of pillage must be put down. To do this, the tribes on the frontier must be reduced to a state of submission... It is a peculiarity of Asiatics to respect nothing but visible and palpable force.[43]

And ruthless force was used. When Russia's World War I mobilization of Kazakh labor inspired uprisings, the revolt was quelled, with 150,000 Kazakhs killed and another 200,000 fleeing to China.

In 1905, Ali Khan Bukeykhanov, a prince and descendant of Jengiz Khan, began the underground intellectual movement Alash Orda as a Kazakh nationalist party. The group tried to gain power in the aftermath of the 1917 Russian Revolution. The Alash Orda sided with the Bolsheviks during the ensuing Civil War that devastated the land and population of Kazakhstan. Alash Orda members were purged from the Kazakh Communist Party during the 1920s, either executed like Ali Khan Bukeykhanov, or exiled to Siberian labor camps.

Under Communist rule, southern Kazakhstan was initially part of the Turkestan Autonomous Soviet Socialist Republic (ASSR), which encompassed most of Soviet Central Asia. A separate ASSR covered northern Kazakhstan, with the capital in Orenburg (now in Russia). The boundaries were changed when the capital moved to Kzyl-Orda (Red Capital) in 1924-25, then to Almaty in 1928. Kazakhstan became a full Soviet Socialist Republic (SSR) in 1936.

Between 1926 and 1933, more than two million Kazakhs died or fled to China as a result of forced collectivization. In the 1930s and 40s, people from other parts of the Soviet Union were settled in Kazakhstan, either as workers for emerging industrial cities or as prisoners in the many labor camps. The latter included whole populations, including Crimean Tatars, Germans, and Muslims from the North Caucasus deported by Stalin during World War II. In addition, many European Soviet citizens, and much of Russia's industry, were moved to Kazakhstan during the war to avoid capture or destruction by Nazi Germany.

In the 1950s, about 800,000 migrants were sent from Russia by Krushchev to create 250,000 square kilometers of agricultural land under the "Virgin Lands" program in northern Kazakhstan. Eventually, Kazakhstan would come to rank third (after Russia and Ukraine) in grain production, and overall represented 18 percent of the USSR's arable land. Other in-migrants from Russia and Ukraine included miners and specialists in the production of coal, oil, iron, and non-ferrous metals.

In the late Soviet period, Kazakhstan became the site of the USSR's space launch center, the Baikonur Cosmodrome, and was its chief nuclear testing ground. Local protests against nuclear testing included riots and demonstrations. Testing was halted in 1989.

# Independent Kazakhstan: 1991 - 2003

At the time of Kazakhstan's independence, Russian was the dominant language in Kazakhstan. Forty percent of the population was Kazakh, 38 percent Russian, five percent Ukrainian and the remaining 17 percent a mixture of other nationalities.[44]

By 2003, things changed significantly. Between 1991 and 2003, over three million ethnic Russians migrated from Kazakhstan to Russia. The Kazakh population in Russia also increased by 600,000 during this same period. The Kazakhs came to Russia for economic reasons and/or because they were political opponents of Kazakh President Nursultan Nazarbayev. While these Kazakhs often remain in their own communities in Russian border towns and are a factor in Kazakh politics, the ethnic Russian immigrants have scattered throughout Russia and have no political organization. For the most part, they stopped caring about Kazakhstan when they left. Although economic factors also influenced their migration, Kazakhstan's policies towards its Russian minority were the primary reason given by over 60 percent of the Russians relocating from Kazakstan.[45] These include:

- Fewer schools using Russian as the language of instruction. Many Russian parents left because they did not want their children to be educated using the Kazakh language. The rise of the Kazakh language s also reflected in a 2001 law man dating that, by 2010, all official signs and government forms must be written in the Kazakh language. Ethnic Russians viewed the imposition of the Kazakh language as anti-Russian because, at the time of independence, 85 percent of the population spoke Russian and only 60 percent of the population spoke Kazakh Of course, from the Kazakh point of view, the primacy of the Kazakh language was central to the stability of their sovereigty.[46]

- Career opportunities for Russians were declining. Despite representing 30 percent of the population, ethnic Russians occupy only seven percent of all management positions (gov ernment and private) in Kazakhstan – and that number is declining.

There are two main reasons given for this dynamic:

1) In some cases, Russian managers have been encouraged to leave, and there is a shortage of qualified Russians for many jobs. This is the result of poor ability to use the Kazakh language and because Russians have difficulty being admitted to professional schools and universities.

2) Such policies are the logical outgrowth of decisions made at the time of independence. As Kazakhstan's Democratic Forces Forum explains:

> During the first phase of statehood building, (creating a unifying idea) of the Kazakh nation was based on the policy of de-Russification and liberation of ethnic Kazakhs from the colonial

> Russian empire. The major objective of the political leadership of this
> multi-ethnic country was to build an ethnically based state...
> [Thus] the political leadership rejected democratic government con
> cepts to accommodate the multi-ethnic composition of the nation.
> None of the four recognized principles of government for regulating
> inter-ethnic issues, such as federalism, the right for proportional rep
> resentation in the government, the state rights of minorities, and the
> right of minorities to participate in the government through coalitions,
> was ever used.[47]

This strategy led not only to the above-discussed flight of ethnic Russians, but also to the drastic reduction or even elimination of non-Kazakhs from public life. For instance, in spite of the fact that ethnic Kazakhs composed only about half of the population, the Kazakh Senate was, in 1999, 100 percent ethnically Kazakh. Further, "once the representatives of the principal ethnic group – the Kazakhs – gained possession of all economic resources, ethnic Russians were removed from important positions in the government sector, economic privatization of government property, and policy making."[48]

Not surprisingly, many of Kazakhstan's ethnically Russian citizens do not like the way their future is evolving. But will they, or Moscow, do anything about it? Or will the Russian settlements in Kazakhstan follow the fate of the Russian communities in China? As late as 1945, there were 50,000 Russians living in Harbin. By 1985, that number had shrunk to 37.[49]

# The Future of Kazakhstan

By 2003, the exodus of Russians from Kazakhstan had slowed considerably. Resettlement centers in Russia's Omsk Oblast (located on the Kazakh border), which had received about 15,000 Russian émigrés from Kazakhstan during each of the peak years of 1993 and 1994, only registered approximately 2,000 Russians who departed in 2002.[50]

In the author's 2003 conversations with ethnic Russians living the northern part of Kazakhstan, there was a consensus that the population of ethnic Russians had stabilized. Of course, people were still leaving, but some who could not find good jobs in Russia were returning. Nevertheless, the exodus of Russians from Kazakhstan has altered the political map. The population of ethnic Russians as a percentage of the total Russian and Kazakh population in urban areas has fallen from 53 percent in 1989 to 39 percent in 1999. The comparable figures for rural areas are 21 percent and 15 percent, respectively. Even in the six border provinces that have the highest concentration of ethnic Russians, the number of those Russians as a percentage of the total Russian and Kazakh population has fallen from 47 percent in 1989 to 44 percent in 1999.[51]

This population decline has precipitated a reduction in Russian nationalist activity in Kazakhstan. Those with the strongest Russian nationalist feelings and those Russians feeling the most aggrieved had left, replaced by Kazakhs immigrating to Kazakhstan from other parts of the former USSR, who usually took the Russians' former homes. These population movements further reduced the proportions of ethnic Russians in the various provinces. Finally, the disproportionately high Kazakh birthrate, and disproportionately old (and therefore not of childbearing years) Russian population, has ensured that the percentage of Russians in all Kazakh regions would continue to decline [See Table 1 below].

## Table 1

**BIRTHS PER 1,000 MINUS DEATHS PER 1,000 IN KAZKHSTAN[52]**

| Ethnic Group | 1959 | 1979 | 1993 |
|---|---|---|---|
| Kazakh | 35.2 | 23.7 | 19.5 |
| Russian | 23.7 | 12.5 | -0.6 |
| Ukrainian | 29.2 | 9.8 | -1.4 |

As a result of this demographic shift, and the increased usage of the Kazakh language, Kazakhstan's northern regions will increasingly look and feel like Kazakhstan – a marked change from 1991, when many of them felt more like Russia.

This change, and an acceptance of political realities, has led to improved relations between Russia and Kazakhstan. In September 2003, both countries joined with Ukraine and Belarus in forming a "Single Economic Space." This agreement states the mutual commitment of all four countries to "synchronize their legislation on tariffs, customs, and transport for the free movement of goods, capital and labor."[53] On the local level, this agreement has strong support. According to Viktor G. Kolpashchikov, Deputy Chair of the Omsk Oblast Administration's Committee on National Politics, Religion and Civil Society, governors on both sides of the Russia/Kazakh border are unanimous in their desire to create a Single Economic Space.[54]

While most approve of this idea for economic reasons, it is supported for another reason as well. For Slavic nationalists, a borderless common economic zone can be seen as a step toward their idea of a greater Slavic State, as witnessed by article four of the draft agreement on the Single Economic Space, which establishes a "single regulatory body" for the four member nations, with the number of votes for each side "premised on its economic potential"[55] - a surefire recipe for Russian dominance.

An expanded Slavic State is also in the minds of the Russian Cossacks. Primarily the descendants of freed serfs who were given lands by the Tsar in

Russian border areas in order to protect the Russian frontier, today's self-identified Cossacks on the Kazakhstan border hope for a new federal Russian law that will, in some measure, reestablish their historic role. This law, which Russian President Putin expects to pass in late 2004 or 2005,[56] would provide money for a Cadet Corps and the establishment of Cossack border settlements. Historically, a Cossack settlement existed every twenty kilometers along the border with smaller settlements at five-kilometer intervals in between.

The reestablishment of these historic Cossack "Kazak Stanitsee" (Cossack villages) would not only help protect the border against drug trafficking, but would surely raise the intensity of the Russian nationalism in the expanded Cossack ranks. Pending the passage of the law, a decree from Russian President Putin gives the Orenburg Cossacks[57] responsibility for protecting part of the Russian-Kazakhstan border.

The vision of an expanded Slavic State exists among some of Kazakhstan's ethnic Russians too. The "LAD" Slavic movement, comprised mainly of Kazakhstan's Cossacks and members of the Communist Party of Kazakhstan, has formally called for a nationwide referendum on the creation of a Kazakhstan-Russia-Belarus Union. Such a move towards union with Russia is one of three choices Anatoli Zubarev, President of the Association of Affiliates of Russian Universities, put forth for Kazakhstan's dissatisfied ethnic Russians.[58] The other choices are to work for internal Kazakh reform and emigration.

However, after traveling on both sides of the Russian-Kazakh border[59] and examining Russian language internet sites, I found no evidence of a critical mass of Russians working toward the inclusion of part of Kazakhstan into Russia. Nor did I find any evidence of a plan to bring about such border changes. At most, there were thoughts that the political environment might change sufficiently for the Kazak Province of East Kazakhstan to become a problem, or that Kazakhstan's relatively passive Russian minority might one day suffer enough to become politically active.[60] Under such scenarios, one or more Kazakh Provinces would announce a referendum to secede from Kazakhstan. The Kazakh government would move to prevent the vote, causing a crisis that would be the pretext for the involvement of the Russian army.

Perhaps with such a situation in mind, in October 2003 Russian Defense Minister Sergei Ivanov proclaimed that Russia might use its military within the CIS if an unstable situation developed or if there were a direct threat to Russian citizens or ethnic Russians.[61] However, expansion of territory is not built on wishful thinking. In the final analysis, the demographic change is likely to be decisive. Barring some large change in the facts on the ground in the not too distant future (e.g., if Russian nationalism is aroused by other parts of the former Soviet Union rejoining association with Moscow is a possibility, particularly in the face of possible Uzbek or Chinese expansion. In that eventuality, a loose confederation with Russia may in fact become a preferred option for Astana, Kazakhstan's capital since 1998.[62]

# MOLDOVA

MOLDOVA
Area: 33,843 Km Sq.
Population: 4,439,502

Major cities:
Chisinau (0.66 Million) capital
Tiraspol (0.19 Million)
Balti (0.15 Million)

# MOLDOVA

## Early History

The territory of present-day Moldova was ruled by Romans, Huns, Ostrogoths, Antes, Bulgarians, Magyars, Pechenegs, Mongols, and Hungarians before the emergence of an independent Moldovan Principality between 1349 and the Ottoman takeover of 1512. The Ottomans ruled until 1792, when they surrendered the present day Dnestr Republic (Transnistria), a Slavic-speaking area, to the Russian Empire under the Treaty of Iasi.

## The Russian and Soviet Eras

Russia's 1792 territorial gains were increased in the aftermath of the Russo-Turkish War of 1806-12. The resulting 1812 Treaty of Bucharest brought Russian sovereignty over Bessarabia, the Romanian-speaking area located between the Dnestr and Prut Rivers.

The limited autonomy enjoyed by Bessarabia between 1812-25 was abolished during the reign of Nicholas I (1825-55). Governmental communication was conducted only in Russian and by 1854 Romanian had lost its status as an official language. The repression of language continued under Tsar Alexander II (1855-81). By 1867, classes were no longer taught in Romanian, and in 1871 churches were forbidden to use Romanian in their services. This transition to the Russian language was facilitated by an immigration of Ukrainians and Russians that more than doubled the total population between 1812 and 1824 alone.[63] The Romanian language continued to survive, however, primarily because the bulk of the Romanian population lived in the countryside where schooling was not a serious pursuit.

In 1917, during the twin turmoils of World War I and the Russian Revolution, Bessarabia announced the creation of an independent Democratic Moldovan Republic to be federated with Russia. However, by February 1918, the Bessarabian leadership had declared the new Republic's complete independence from Moscow. Two months later, they decided instead to unite with Romania.

In 1924, the newly-formed Soviet government established the Moldovan Autonomous Oblast on the territory east of the Dnestr River in the Ukrainian SSR. The new Oblast's capital was Balta, now located in Ukraine. In 1929, the capital was moved to Tiraspol, now the capital of the self-named Dnestr Republic. In violation of international norms as well as its pact with Nazi Germany, the Soviet Union unilaterally occupied Bessarabia in June of 1940. By August of that year, the Soviets had created the Moldovan SSR, unifying most of Bessarabia with a slice of the Moldovan Autonomous Oblast. The Ukraine SSR was able to claim the remainder of the Oblast, plus additional territory from Romania. In 1941, sovereignty again shifted as Nazi and Romanian troops regained the territory, only to surrender it to the Soviet Union in August 1944. Soviet sovereignty over these territories was formally recognized by Romania in the Paris peace treaties of 1947.[64]

Post-World War II Soviet Moldova was characterized by the deportation of approximately 500,000 Romanians between 1944 and 1970 (offset by the settlement of a comparable number of non-Romanians) and the domination of the Moldovan government and Communist party by Slavs. For instance, in 1979, Slavs in Moldova numbered 27 percent of the population but held 65 percent of the ministerial posts.[65]

By 1989, Moldovans who identified themselves as Romanians had gained sufficient power to make Romanian an official language. In response, ethnic Slavs – especially in the territory of today's "Dnestr Republic" – organized to protect Slavic interests.

1990 witnessed the formation of the Gagauz Republic (dominated by Moldova's Turkic-speaking minority) and the Dnestr Republic (dominated by Moldova's Slavic-speaking minority). Although Moldova's Supreme Soviet (their legislature) voted to nullify these declarations, it had no effect on the Dnestr Republic's movement toward *de facto* independence.

# Independent Moldova: 1991-2003

The last pre-independence census (conducted in 1989) showed a population of 4.3 million – 64 percent Moldovan (ethnically Romanian), 14 percent Ukrainian, 13 percent Russian, and the remaining nine percent coming from the Gagauz nationality (Christian Turks) and other minority groups.[66]

Moldova's August 27, 1991 declaration of independence from the crumbling USSR was followed by a grant of unconditional citizenship to all permanent residents, regardless of nationality.[67] Nevertheless, the issue of Russian identity remained a divisive one. Throughout the decade that followed, political tensions between nationalist groups, like the Popular Front of Moldova, which advocates Moldova's unification with Romania, and the Russia-centric Communist Party of Moldova, played a major role in Moldovan national politics.[68] This tension has been exacerbated in recent years by the successful efforts of pro-Russian groups to make Russian-language instruction mandatory in the Moldovan educational system[69] – a move taken despite the fact that only one-third of Moldovans speak Russian as a first language.

# The Question of the Dnestr Republic

Following the December 1991 election of Igor Smirnov as the Dnestr Republic's President, 50,000 armed Moldovan nationalists descended upon the breakaway Republic. Violence was kept to a minimum only through the intervention of Russia's 14th Army, formerly the Soviet 14th Army. Fighting, however, began anew in 1992 and was once again stopped through the intercession of the 14th Army under the command of General Alexandr Lebed. The resulting cease-fire agreement included the following provisions:

- that forces from Russia, Moldova, and the Dnestr Republic would maintain the demarcation line;
- that Moscow agreed to remove the 14th Army provided suitable constitutional guarantees were given to the Dnestr Republic; and
- that the Dnestr Republic would have the right to secede if Moldova united with Romania.

Russia's post-Lebed connection with the Dnestr Republic remains strong. Russia continues to train young officers from the Transdniester forces and Russian citizenship is widely held among the Transdniester leadership. A December 1999 OSCE agreement, known as the Istanbul Accords, mandated the removal of all Moldovan-based Russian forces by December 2002. When it was clear that Russia would not meet its commitment, a new deadline was set for December 2003. On December 3, 2003, Russian Foreign Minister Igor Ivanov explained the continuing presence of Russian troops:

> Russia always has carried out its obligations and continues to do
> so. When it comes to the armed forces in Moldova... the Istanbul
> Accords envisaged holding relevant talks to find a solution to
> both these issues. These talks are taking place. Unfortunately, the
> fact that the situation is unsettled in Moldova... is a serious
> impediment to completing these talks.[70]

But the November 17, 2000 *Nezavisimaya Gazeta* provided another explanation for Russia's reluctance to remove the troops: "A new policy (of) the Russian President is aimed at increasing Russia's political and economic influence in the Dnestr region... The current leadership of the Russian Federation... has realized the importance the Dnestr region... both economically and in a military and strategic sense."[71]

# The Future of Transdniester

Since late 1992, Transdniester authorities have proposed a confederation of two equal states as the solution to its conflict with the rest of Moldova. Failing this, they threaten to declare independence from Moldova. In 1996, newly-named Russian Foreign Minister Yevgenni Primakov began supporting this idea of "Common states" for Moldova-Transdniester. It was anticipated that such an agreement would also provide for Russian becoming an official language in Moldova and for the continued presence of Russian troops in Transdniester.

After a decade of *de facto* independence, Transdniester's leadership has joined that of Russia, Moldova and the OSCE in the search for a resolution of their incompatible claims of sovereignty over Transdniester. A recent report by *Radio Free Europe/Radio Liberty* succinctly described the nature of the July 2002-February 2003 negotiations:

> On 9 July 2002, Moldovan newspapers published the draft of a document drawn up by Russia, Ukraine and the OSCE to create a federal Moldovan state in which autonomous territories (including the Transdniester) would be allowed their own legislatures and constitutions. In reality, this and subsequent drafts go further than a federation and create a virtual confederation of the two states.[72]

Nationalist Moldovan opposition has, thus far, prevented Moldovan President Vladimir Voronin from signing this document. This status quo is likely to remain.

Russian expansionists hope that, either with a federation as a first step or without it, independence will eventually become a reality – followed by a referendum in which Transdniesterian voters will request annexation by Russia. Such a request was envisioned by the authors of the law reproduced in Appendix I, when they provided the path by which part of a state non-contiguous to the Russian Federation could become part of the Russian Federation. A variation of this idea has Moldova dissolving as a state, with the Dnestr Republic going to Russia and the remainder becoming part of Romania.

But since the Gagauz Republic would vehemently resist incorporation into Romania, any plan that does not take its interests into consideration cannot be taken seriously.

Meanwhile, some Ukrainian officials, including Volodymyr Litvyn, Speaker of the Rada, Ukraine's lower legislative body, feel that if Transdniester leaves Moldova it is likely to join Ukraine.[73] While this may make geographic sense, the reality of a Russian (not Ukrainian) troop presence in Transdniester suggests that there is little chance of Kiev gaining sovereignty over the area under current conditions.

# UKRAINE

Area: 603,700 Km Sq.
Population: 48,055,439

Major cities:
Kiev (2.61 Million) capital
Kharkiv (1.47 Million)
Dnipropetrovsk (1.07 Million)

# UKRAINE

## Early History

The beginnings of the Ukrainian nation can be traced to the arrival of Slavic tribes in the territory of present-day central and eastern Ukraine in the 6th Century. By the 11th Century, the state of Kiev Rus', founded in 862 and converted to Christianity in 988, was geographically the largest state in Europe. The 13th Century, however, saw much of Kiev destroyed by Mongol raiders.

In the wake of the Mongol retreat, Poland and Lithuania moved during the 14th Century to annex most of territory of Ukraine. In 1654, an increasingly powerful Russia gained sovereignty over much of Ukrainian territory. The remainder stayed under Polish control until the second and third partitions of Poland (1772 and 1793, respectively), when almost all of it also became part of the Russian Empire. The period of Polish control is responsible for a good deal of the current difference between the Russian and Ukrainian languages.

## The Russian and Soviet Eras

The two centuries of Russian and Soviet rule were characterized by multiple, and ultimately unsuccessful, efforts to destroy Ukrainian nationalism. These "Russification" programs can be divided into four basic categories:

## Church Conversion

In the 1770s, Catherine the Great began a program to destroy the power of the Uniate Church.[74] State powers were used to convert Uniates to Russian Orthodoxy. The Orthodox Church "became an instrument of Russification and a foremost representative of the official imperial ideology, with glorification of the Tsar, Orthodoxy, and Russian Nationality."[75]

Following Catherine's death in 1796, Tsars Paul I (1796-1801) and Alexander I (1801-1825) reversed this policy. Nicholas I (1825-55), however, strongly embraced Catherine's policy, and by 1839 the Uniate metropolitanate was abolished and the Uniates were absorbed into the Russian Orthodox Church. Five hundred and ninety-three of 1,898 Uniate clergy refused the conversion and were exiled to the interior of Russia or Siberia.[76]

But the eradication of a belief is a difficult undertaking. During more than

100 years of Russian or Soviet control, the Uniate Church lived underground, emerging only in the late 1980s as "demands grew for the relegalization of this Eastern rite Catholic Church. Defections by the clergy and entire congregations from Russian Orthodoxy began in the fall of 1989."[77]

The Ukrainian Orthodox Church also felt the pressures of "Russification." It formally became a part of the Russian Orthodox structure and, between 1799 and the early 1970s, no Tsar or Soviet Leader appointed an ethnic Ukrainian as Metropolitian of Kiev. As a result, the church became, among other things, a vehicle for spreading the Russian language.

## Repression of the Ukrainian Language

In 1863, Russia's Minister of the Interior, Pyotr Valuev, banned virtually all Ukrainian language publications. The ban was reinforced by a secret imperial decree of Alexander II in 1876, the Ems Ukaz, and included a ban on the importation of Ukrainian books or public readings and stage performances in the language. The prohibition extended to education, a major contributing factor to the low rate of literacy among Ukrainians – which stood at only 13 percent in 1897.[78]

The failure of the 1905 revolution, and a related March 1905 decision by the Russian Academy of Sciences that Ukrainian was not a Russian dialect, but an independent language, led to reforms that relaxed the restrictions on the use of the Ukrainian language.[79] Russian continued to be the only language of instruction in schools. The anarchy caused by the revolution of 1917 led – albeit temporarily – to the free use the Ukrainian language. Ukrainian even became the official state language in the early 1920s. But the beginning of the Soviet period saw Russian reemerge as the language of all official communications of the Ukrainian Communist Party and the government of the Ukrainian SSR.

The use of the Ukrainian language continued in other places. As late as 1933, 88 percent of all students in Soviet Ukraine were receiving instruction in Ukrainian.[80] That number would increase slightly in the years that followed, but the systemic decline of Ukrainian language use had begun. In 1933, Mykola Skrypnyk, Ukraine's Commissioner of Education, reportedly committed suicide after being officially accused of "alienating the Ukrainian Language from Russian."[81] His successors instituted a new policy designed to alter the vocabulary, alphabet and grammar of the Ukrainian language in a way that would permit its eventual merger into the unchanged Russian language. New education reforms were designed to ensure that all Ukrainians would have fluency in Russian. By 1938, the study of Russian had become mandatory in all schools.

By 1988, the percentage of elementary school students enrolled in Ukrainian language schools had shrunk to 48 percent.

Nevertheless, in 1989, 65 percent of Ukrainian citizens spoke Ukrainian as their first language, compared to 33 percent whose first language was Russian. Seventy-six percent spoke both languages.[82]

## Repression of Ukrainians and Russian Migration

Under the Tsar, repression of Ukrainian nationalists usually meant exile, perhaps preceded by a year or two in jail. However, conditions were not so easy in the USSR. Soviet repression of "harmful nationalism" was especially severe and, in addition to language restrictions, the deportation and killing of intellectuals was common. Between 1932-33, a Stalin-engineered famine killed as many as seven million people in Ukraine. Many of their homes were soon filled by ethnic Russians who had been encouraged, for both economic and political reasons, to move to Ukraine.

Between war and political killings in the first half of the twentieth century, Ukraine may have lost as much as one-half of its male population and one-quarter of its female population.[83] Ukraine's cultural elite suffered disproportionately, with around 80 percent either killed or sent to camps during the 1930s alone.[84]

In the aftermath of World War II "Sovietization," nearly a half million people (including the entire populations of some villages) from the newly-acquired Western Territories of Ukraine were deported to Siberia and Central Asia. They were replaced by 327,000 Russians. The Russian population in the Western Territories, which was almost nonexistent at the end of World War II, had reached five percent by 1959.[85]

Repression and/or migration also involved those who were not ethnically Ukrainian. Pursuant to Soviet agreements with Poland and Czechoslovakia, 1.3 million Poles were repatriated to Poland – and 53,000 Czechs to Czechoslovakia – between 1945 and 1948. Under the same agreements, 500,000 Ukrainians returned to Ukraine from Poland, and 12,000 from Czechoslovakia.[86] Additionally, Tatars (90 percent of Crimea's 1783 population) had, by 1987, "dropped to thirty-four percent primarily as a result of Stalin's 1944 deportation of Tatars to Central Asia and their replacement with ethnic Russians."[87]

## Russian Control of Political and Military Power

During the period of Tsarist control, all major political appointments were made by the Tsar. However, much of the local administration in Ukraine was carried out by local noblemen. Between 1790 and 1835, tens of thousands of Ukrainians (mostly Cossack officers) were declared nobles under Catherine the Great's 1785 Charter of Nobility. That meant, among other things, that they had the right to trial by peers, were exempt from paying taxes, could avoid forced government service, and were allowed to own serfs.

Ethnic Ukrainians' influence during this period was weak in the cities and, therefore, in the fields of commerce and political power. In 1897, 72 percent (17 million) of the population of Dnieper Ukraine were ethnic Ukrainians,[88] while ethnic Ukrainians numbered only 34 percent of the urban population (vs. 34 percent Russian and 27 percent Jewish).

While Ukrainian political officeholders existed under the Tsars, the Russian monopoly on military power in Ukraine was unquestioned. This factor is often cited in explaining the failure of the attempts to create an independent Ukrainian state in 1918-1919.

Still, many had hopes for Ukrainian autonomy under Communist rule until a December 1920 treaty subordinated all ministers of Ukraine to those in Moscow. A more formal structure was put in place with the 1922 founding of the Soviet Union.

Ukrainians, then 80 percent of the population, constituted less than 20 percent of the Communist Party (Bolshevik) of Ukraine (CPBU) in 1920.[89] This number would rise to 50 percent in the late 1920s, and 60 percent by 1959. Regardless of the percentage, however, Russians always held control. These policies were liberalized under the rule of Ukraine Party boss Petro Shelest, but his successor Vlodymyr Shcherbyts'ky did his best to repress Ukrainian culture, nationalism and political power.

# Territorial Changes

Western Ukraine declared its independence from Austro-Hungary in November 1917, a move that was mirrored by a central/eastern Ukrainian declaration of independence from Russia in January of the following year. After a brief period of separate sovereignty (punctuated by the annexation of Crimea to the central Ukrainian state), the two halves united on January 22, 1919.

The Poles captured Kiev in May 1920, before surrendering it to the Bolsheviks just one month later. The Polish/Bolshevik line had stabilized by 1921, when part of present-day western Ukraine came under Polish rule. At that time, the central and eastern parts of the country became part of the Soviet Union. All this territory returned to the Soviet Union as a result of its 1939 invasion of Poland, but shortly thereafter was lost to the Nazis. The USSR again regained the territory in the aftermath of World War II.

Additional territory was added as well. In 1945, the USSR annexed the largely Ukrainian-speaking Carpatho-Ukraine district of pre-World War II Czechoslovakia. It was the first time this territory had been under either Soviet or Russian sovereignty.

A final addition to Ukrainian territory came through a move that, at the time, seemed purely administrative. In 1954, Soviet leader Nikita Krushchev took the Crimean Oblast from the territory of the Russian SSR and gave it to the Ukrainian SSR.

# The Struggle for Autonomy and Sovereignty

In her book *Ukraine*, Marta Dyczok identifies three occasions in the Soviet era when Ukraine made a serious bid for autonomy and/or independence. The first occurred in the 1920s, when many believed in the possibility of a truly federal state. This belief disappeared with Stalin's centralization of power. A second opportunity came with Petro Shelest's 1963 rise to the head of Ukraine's Communist Party. Shelest "attempted to re-define relations with Moscow and took steps to assert economic, cultural and political autonomy."[90] Eventually, Shelest went too far for Moscow's taste. The 1972 Brezhnev crackdown removed Shelest and his supporters from power in the Communist Party of Ukraine. Shelest's replacement, Volodymyr Shcherbyts'kyi, quashed nationalist aspirations until his fall from power in 1989. Dyczok marks the Gorbachev era as the beginning of the third and successful bid. It succeeded because the local elite wanted the power that comes with independence and saw an opportunity to take it in the aftermath of the failed coup attempt in Moscow, and because omnipresent Ukrainian nationalist sentiments were increasingly inflamed as Ukrainians suffered economically and ecologically (Chernobyl) under the policies of Gorbachev. The almost universal feeling was that Ukraine could do better on its own.

In July 1990, the Ukrainian parliament passed the Declaration on Sovereignty. In a March 1991 referendum, Ukrainians gave 71 percent of their vote for the preservation of the USSR while simultaneously casting 80 percent of their votes for maximizing Ukrainian autonomy.

On August 24, 1991, just days after the failed 1991 coup attempt in Moscow, independence was declared in Kiev. The same day, the Parliament of Ukraine drafted a motion to take control of troops stationed on Ukraine's territory. In a referendum that December, 92 percent of the population of Ukraine voiced their approval for the declaration of independence. Even 51 percent of the heavily Russified Crimea supported independence.

# Independent Ukraine: 1991-2003

The first years of Ukrainian independence saw an outpouring of nationalist sentiments in Russia. In July 1993, the Russian Supreme Soviet (then Russia's parliament) proclaimed the Ukrainian port of Sevastopol to be Russian. Similar statements came from Moscow Mayor Yuri Luzhkov and other prominent political figures, but Russian President Boris Yeltsin and his Foreign Minister Andrei Kozyrev quickly denounced the Supreme Soviet's decision. World opinion was clear. A 1993 UN Security Council resolution called upon the Supreme Soviet to renounce its claim on Sevastopol.

When the Russian-Ukrainian border question was resolved with the signing of a May 1997 treaty, many major Russian figures still could not reconcile themselves to the treaty's territorial provisions. More than a year later, in October 1998, Mayor Luzkhov emotionally proclaimed on Russian television that:

> Sevastopol is a Russian city and Crimea is a Russian land. Even when Khrushchev transferred Crimea (to Ukraine) Sevastopol was not part of Crimea in administrative terms. It was a separate administrative entity, which was directly subordinate to the USSR government... Sevastopol is a Russian city and will remain a Russian city.[91]

Ukraine's internal political response to lingering Russian claims on its territory has, in some ways, been a mirror image of Russian and Soviet policies during their years of control. Study of the Ukrainian language is mandatory. The fortunes of the Ukrainian Orthodox Church and the Uniate Church are rising in comparison to those parishes loyal to the Russian Orthodox Church. Ethnic Russians can hold political positions but, in the aggregate, are not trusted to control Ukraine's destiny.

Still, Russia is increasing its economic (and, therefore, political) influence in Ukraine. This has been accomplished in two ways. First, Russia has concluded bilateral agreements – especially in the energy sector – that strategically benefit Russia. One example is the 2002 agreement permitting Moscow to pay "energy transit fees with gas instead of rubles," a move which reduced "commercial revenues" while simultaneously increasing Ukraine's "already heavy reliance on Russian gas."[92] Second, in September 2003, Russia persuaded Ukraine to join the Russian-promoted and dominated "Single Economic Space" (SES) of Russia, Belarus, and Kazakhstan.

Politically, Russia's leverage has also been bolstered by the rising tensions that have characterized relations between the Kuchma government and its opposition since the spring of 2003. As part of this escalating tug-of-war, the Kuchma government has proposed a series of controversial constitutional measures aimed at allowing the current Ukrainian president to retain power through parliamentary means. These moves have simultaneously diminished the Kuchma administration's credibility at home and nudged it closer to the Kremlin on international issues.

# The Future of Ukraine

Ukraine today faces a profound dilemma: "Russia remains both the main threat to (Ukraine's) statehood and its main trading partner."[93]

The chances of Ukraine drawing closer (through more fully integrated economies, greater strategic cooperation, etc.) to Russia improve proportional to:

- the acquisition of major industries in Ukraine by ethnic Russians on the Ukrainian side of the border;
- whether, and how, Russia is able to advance the political careers of pro-Moscow Ukrainians;
- dimming memories of Chernobyl and other Soviet-created catastrophes and;
- the creation of the agreed-upon regulatory body of the SES -- a move that would subordinate parts of Ukraine's economic sovereignty to that organ.

But closeness is not a union, and any attempts at union or Russia's annexation of part of Ukraine's territory would be met by force. The Ukrainian nationalists are prepared to fight. Given this reality, even a nationalist Russian government would be unlikely to attempt a territorial grab in the foreseeable future. But the passage of time creates opportunities that even the best of pundits cannot foresee. This is the last hope of those Russians wishing to bring Ukraine under Moscow's control.

# Conclusion

Russia's military, economic and diplomatic power has been used successfully by Vladimir Putin to increase Russian influence in Belarus, Ukraine, Georgia, Kazakhstan and Moldova. Concurrently, the Kremlin has succeeded in laying the basis for further influence or even possible future annexation through a variety of levers, chief among them:

1) The passage of a 2001 law defining the procedure for another country or territory to join the Russian Federation (Appendix I);
2) The Russian Defense Ministry's 2003 policy legitimizing the use of force to protect Russian citizens abroad; and, Prime Minister Mikhail Fradkov's articulated goal of simplifying grants of citizenship to ethnic Russians living abroad; and
3) The creation of a Single Economic Space encompassing Belarus, Kazakhstan, Russia and Ukraine.

At least in the near term, there is every reason to believe that Russia will continue such policies in a largely peaceful fashion. Even the most fervent Russian nationalists understand the difficulty of expansion.

Nevertheless, the idea of a Greater Russia continues to animate policymakers in Moscow. As influential politicians like Duma Deputy Chairman Dmitry Rogozin make clear, Russia must work actively to "create conditions" necessary for a union with its former satellites, "no matter how unrealistic" such an idea appears today.[94]

The chances for such an enlargement will decrease over time, and with the steadfastness of the world's (especially the West's) determination to prevent any unilateral change of borders. Such chances will increase with the first annexation, however small, of new territory. And they will become more probable to the degree that Russian assistance – be it in the fight against terrorism, achieving energy security, or a host of other contemporary issues – is viewed as vital to Western strategic interests. Simply put, one day, Russia's partnership with the West may be judged as more important than its annexation of former Soviet territories.

# Notes

[1] "Fact Sheet: Independent States in the World," United States Department of State, Bureau of Intelligence and Research, Washington, DC, 27 Feb. 2004. Found online at http://www.state.gov/s/inr/rls/4250.htm.

[2] "Treaty of Trianon," *Encyclopedia Britannica*, 2004 edition. Found online at http://www.britannica.com/eb/article?eu=75247.

[3] "Background Note: Hungary," United States Department of State, Bureau of European and Eurasian Affairs, Nov. 2003. Found online at http://www.state.gov/r/pa/ei/bgn/26566.htm.

[4] Arnaud de Borchgrave, "Regime change… a la carte," *Washington Times*, 18 Mar. 2003.

[5] "Background Notes: Italy," United States Department of State, Bureau of European and Eurasian Affairs, Jan. 2004. Found online at http://www.state.gov/r/pa/ei/bgn/4033.htm.

[6] Ilan Berman and Herman Pirchner, "Reviving Greater Russia," *Washington Times*, 24 Oct. 2002.

[7] Appendix I, Chapter I, Article 4.1.

[8] Appendix I, Chapter II, Article 6.1.

[9] "Noviye Primyer Rossii Mikhail Fradkov podelil pravitelstvo na 3 urovnia i obeshal ulutshit zhizn," NEWSru.com, 5 Mar. 2004. Found online at http://www.newsru.com/arch/russia/05Mar2004/frad.html.

[10] Alexandr Solzhenitsyn, *The Russian Question* (New York: Farrar, 1995) 89.

[11] Ibid., 93.

[12] Dmitry Rogozin, *Muy Vernyom Sebe Rossiyu* (We Will Reclaim Russia for Ourselves), Official website of Dmitry Rogozin, 2003. Available online, in Russian, at http://www.rogozin.ru/book/297.

[13] "Poll indicates most Russians, Ukrainians, Belarussians favor reunification," *RIA Novosti*, 5 Jan. 2001.

[14] Andrew Jack, "Putin 'could stay in power as head of post-Soviet confederation,'" *Financial Times*, 28 Oct. 2003.

[15] U.S. Department of State, *Belarus and Moldova: country studies* (Washington, DC: Government Printing Office, 1995) 15-17.

[16] Steve Gutterman, "Putin suggests a full union with Belarus is possible, Belarussian leader rejects idea," *Associated Press*, 14 Aug. 2002.

[17] "Annexation of Georgia in Russian Empire (1801-1878)," Official website of the Parliament of the Republic of Georgia, n.d. Found online at http://www.parliament.ge/GENERAL/HISTORY/his9.html.

[18] Cited in the *Washington Post*, 3 Dec. 2003.

[19] Niko Mchedlishvili, "Georgia warned by Russia, defended by US, on base," *Reuters*, 13 Jan. 2004.

[20] Russian Ministry of Foreign Affairs, Information and Press Department, *Daily News Bulletin*, 16 Jan. 2004. Found online at http://www.ln.mid.ru/.

[21] "Georgia: The Balkans of the 21st Century," *Nezavisimaya Gazeta*, 25 Nov. 2003.

[22] Ajaria was first incorporated into the Russian Empire in 1878, when it was conquered from the Ottoman Empire by the Russian imperial armies. Having converted to Islam in the 16th and the 17th centuries, Ajarians became a minority in predominantly Christian Georgia. Under Russian imperial rule, Georgia went through a national awakening – focusing attention on Ajaria and its adherence to Islam as an "aberration" that had to be "eradicated through national enlightenment." In the period between the collapse of the Russian Empire and the Bolshevik Revolution, Georgia attempted to foment this "national enlightenment," but was met with resistance from rebellious Muslim Ajarians supported by the Turkish military. The Bolsheviks annexed Georgia in 1921, and granted Ajaria special autonomous status within the Georgian Soviet Socialist Republic. George Katsiaficas, ed. *After the Fall: 1989 and the Future of Freedom* (New York: Routledge, 2001) 106-109.

[23] Author's interview with Rezo Shamilishvili, head of the Ajarian Council of Administrators, Batumi, Georgia, 31 Jan. 2004. In his remarks, Shamilishvili indicated that some accommodation with the newly-elected President Saakashvili was possible.

[24] Author's interview with Georgian National Security Council Deputy Director Nikoloz Vashakidze, Tbilisi, Georgia, 29 Jan. 2004.

[25] "Facts and Figures," Official website of the United Nations Observer Mission to Georgia, n.d. Found online at http://www.unomig.org/facts_and_figures/facts_and_figures.asp.

[26] "Georgian nationalists demand pull-out of Russian troops from Abkhazia," *Agence France Presse*, 2 July 2003.

[27] Zbigniew Brzezinski, "The Premature Partnership," *Foreign Affairs*, Mar.-Apr. 1994: 69.

[28] Liana Kvarchelia, "An Abkhaz Perspective," *Conciliation Resources*, 3 Oct. 2003. Found online at http://www.c-r.org/accord/geor-ab/accord7/abkhaz.shtml.

[29] United Nations, Security Council, S/Res/1096, 30 Jan. 1997. Archived online at http://www.hri.ca/fortherecord1997/documentation/security/s-res-1096.htm.

[30] "Georgian President adheres to Policy of Dialogue with Russian President," *Georgian Radio* (Tbilisi), 15 July 2002.

[31] Justin Burke, "Georgian president censures Russian citizenship bill," Eurasianet.org, 11 June 2002. Found online at http://www.eurasianet.org/resource/georgia/hypermail/200206/0015.shtml.

[32] Author's interview with Abkhaz Foreign Minister Sergei Shamba, Sochi, Russia, 27 Jan. 2004.

[33] Author's interview with Deputy Chairman of the Georgian Parliament Vakhtang Rcheulishvili, Tbilisi, Georgia, 24 Sept. 2003.

[34] Interview with Abkhaz Foreign Minister Sergei Shamba.

[35] Nikola Cvetkovski, "The Georgian-South Ossetian Conflict," diss., Aalborg University, n.d. Found online at http://www.caucasus.dk/chapter4.htm.

[36] Open Society Institute, *Forced Migration: Repatriation in Georgia*, July 1995. Found online at http://www2.soros.org/fmp2/html/georgia.htm.

[37] Yevgeniy Verlin, "South Ossetia's Kokoiti Interview," *Nezavisimaya Gazeta*, 27 Nov. 2003. [38] "Georgia's Breakaway Region of South Ossetia Hopes to Join Russian Federation." *Prime-News*, 5 July 2002. [39] Kevarchelia, "An Abkhaz Perspective." [40] "Leader of Georgia's Breakaway Ossetia Region Seeks Russian Support," *Imedi TV* (Tbilisi), 27 Nov. 2003.

[41] Author's interview with Caucasian Institute President David Darchiasvilli, Tblisi, Georgia, 30 Jan. 2004.

[42] Adilbek N. Begedaev, *Kazakhstan: diagrama istorichiskogo rozvitiya gossudarstva* (Kazakhstan: Diagram of historical governmental evolution) (Almaty: AdalBusinessPrint, 2003).

[43] James Cracraft, *Major Problems in the History of Imperial Russia* (Lexington: D.C. Heath and Company, 1994) 410-1.

[44] Appendix (Table 6) in G. Baratova et al., eds. *History of Kazakhstan* – Peoples and Cultures, (Almaty: Daik Press, 2001) 596-597.

[45] Author's interview with the staff of the Committee on the CIS and Contacts with Compatriots of the Russian State Duma, Moscow, Russia, 17 Apr. 2003.

[46] This policy mirrors language politics in the Baltic States, Ukraine, and other parts of the former USSR.

[47] "Russians in Kazakhstan: Challenges and Prospects at the Dawn of the New Century," Official website of Kazakhstan's Democratic Forces Forum, 11 Mar. 2003. Found online at http://forumkz.org/article/izb_27_03_02_1.htm.

[48] *Ibid.*

[49] John F. Burns, "Russian Legacy Fades in North China," *New York Times*, 11 Aug. 1985.

[50] Author's interview with Kazakhstan Committee on National Politics, Religion and Civil Society Deputy Chair Viktor G. Kolpashnikov, Omsk, Kazakhstan, 18 Apr. 2003.

[51] Republic of Kazakhstan, State Agency on Statistics, *Collection of Statistics on the Republic of Kazakhstan* (Almaty: Informatsionno-Vycheslitelny Tsentr Agenstva Respubliki Kazakhstan Statistike, 2000).

[52] Kazakh Academy of Sciences, Institute of History and Ethnology, *History of Kazakhstan – Essays* (Almaty: Gylym Publishing, 1998) 187.

[53] Mara D. Bellaby, "Ex-Soviet Republics OK Free-Trade Zone," *Anchorage Daily News*, 19 Sept. 2003.

[54] Interview with Viktor G. Kolpashnikov.

[55] Appendix II, Article 4.

[56] "Putin in Live Phone-In Answers Citizens' Questions," *RTR TV* (Moscow), 18 Dec. 2003.

[57] One of three major regional Cossack organizations.

[58] "Russians in Kazakhstan: Challenges and Prospects at the Dawn of the New Century."

[59] Author's travels in southern Russia, April 2003 and northern Kazakhstan, July 2003.

[60] Author's interview with Kazakhstan Institute for Strategic Studies Director Maulen S. Ashimbaev, Almaty, Kazakhstan, 25 Jul. 2003.

[61] "Defense Minister Says Russia Could Use Force to Defend its Compatriots in CIS," *Radio Free Europe/Radio Liberty Newsline*, 6 Oct. 2003. Found online at http://www.rferl.org/newsline/2003/10/1-RUS/rus-061003.asp.

[62] Kazakh President Nursultan Nazarbayev officially relocated the capital of Kazakhstan from Almaty to Akmola in 1998. Akmola was subsequently renamed Astana, also by presidential order. *Agence France Presse*, 7 May 1998.

[63] Markus Schonherr, "Russification and Ethnic Consciousness of Romanians in

Bessarabia (1812 to 1991)," diss. Budapest University of Economics, n.d. Found online at http://www.east-west-wg.org/cst/cst-mold/bessara.html.

[64] Organization for Security and Cooperation in Europe, OSCE Conflict Prevention Centre, *Transdniestrian Conflict – Origins and Issues*, Official Website of the Organization For Cooperation and Security in Europe, 10 Jun. 1994. Found online at http://www.osce.org/moldova/documents/files/background.pdf.

[65] Schonherr, "Russification and Ethnic Consciousness of Romanians in Bessarabia (1812 to 1991)."

[66] "Country Profile: Moldova," *Economist Intelligence Unit* 1996, 37.

[67] Eugen Tomiuc, "Moldova: Minority Report – Russian Speakers a Minority but Russian Language Rules," *Radio Free Europe/Radio Liberty*, 21 Aug. 2003. Found online at http://www.rferl.org/features/2003/08/21082003160351.asp.

[68] "Developments in Moldova since 1990," Website of the European Forum, February 1997. Found online at http://www/europeanforum.bot-consult.se/cup/moldova.

[69] Eugen Tomiuc, "Moldova: Education Officials Introduce Russian as Mandatory Foreign Language," *Radio Free Europe/Radio Liberty*, 21 Dec. 2001. Found online at http://www.rferl.org/features/2001/12/21122001104851.asp.

[70] "Russia and NATO Step Away From Potential Deterioration in Relations," *NTV Mir* (Moscow), 4 Dec. 2003.

[71] Natalya Kamchatova, "The 'Unity of the Dnestr Region' Public Movement Is a Key Link Between the Unrecognized Republic and Russia," *Nezavisimaya Gazeta*, 17 Nov. 2000.

[72] Taras Kuzio, "Is Federalization the Right Option for Moldova?" *RFE/RL Newsline*, 10 Mar. 2003. Found online at http://www.rferl.org/newsline/2003/03/100303.asp.

[73] Author's interview, Washington, DC, 24 Sept. 2003.

[74] Eastern rite Christian churches, predominantly of Eastern Europe and the Middle East, that enjoy full communion with the Roman Catholic Church, but retain their own liturgical practices and discipline.

[75] Paul R. Magocsi, *History of Ukraine* (Toronto: University of Toronto Press, 1996) 375.

[76] *Ibid.*

[77] "Short History of Ukraine," *Vesti* (Bergen: University of Bergen, n.d.). Found online at http://www.hf.uib.no/Andre/vesti/ukrainehistory.htm.

[78] Ibid.

[79] Hugh Seton-Watson, *The Russian Empire: 1801-1917* (New York: Oxford University Press, 1967) 608.

[80] Magocsi, *History of Ukraine*, 564.

[81] *Ibid.*, 567.

[82] *Itogi Vsesoiuznoi perepisi naseleniia 1989 goda*, Vol. 7, Ch. 1 (1989) 10.

[83] "History of Ukraine," *Lonely Planet World Guide*, 30 Nov. 2003. Found online at http://www.lonelyplanet.com/destinations/europe/ukraine/history.htm.

[84] "Short History of Ukraine."

[85] Magocsi, *History of Ukraine*, 651.

[86] *Ibid.* 642.

[87] Marta Dyczok, *Ukraine: Movement without change, change without movement* (Amsterdam, The Netherlands: Harwood, 2000) 18.

[88] Magosci, *History of Ukraine*, 331-2.

[89] "Short History of Ukraine."

[90] Dyczok, *Ukraine: Movement without change, change without movement*, 48.

[91] "Moscow Mayor Luzhkov on Relations with Communists, status of Crimea." *Russian Public TV* (Moscow), 31 Oct. 1998.

[92] Ilan Berman, "Sliding Back into Moscow's Orbit," *International Herald Tribune*, 5 Nov. 2003.

[93] Dyczok, *Ukraine: Movement without change, change without movement*, 105.

[94] Rogozin, *Muy Vernyom Sebe Rossiyu* (We Will Reclaim Russia for Ourselves).

# Appendix I
# Law on the Expansion of the Russian Federation

Consistent with Article 65, Part 2, of the Constitution of the Russian Federation, this Federal Constitutional Law establishes the main conditions and procedure for accepting new Russian Federation entities into the Russian Federation or forming such entities therein.

## Chapter I. General

### Article 1. Basic Concepts Used in This Federal Constitutional Law

1. Acceptance of a new federation entity into the Russian Federation is a procedure envisioning a change in the composition of Russian Federation entities resulting from joining a foreign state, or a part thereof, to the Russian Federation.
2. Formation of a new federation entity in the Russian Federation is a procedure envisioning a change in the composition of Russian Federation entities in compliance with this Federal Constitutional Law that does not involve acceptance of a foreign state, or a part thereof, into the Russian Federation.

### Article 2. Russian Federation Laws on Acceptance of New Federation Entities into the Russian Federation or Forming Such Entities Therein

1. Acceptance of new federation entities into the Russian Federation shall be effected in consistence with the Constitution of the Russian Federation, international (interstate) treaties of the Russian Federation, this Federal Constitutional Law, as well as federal constitutional laws on accepting new federation entities into the Russian Federation.
2. Formation of a new federation entity in the Russian Federation shall be effected in consistence with the Constitution of the Russian Federation, this Federal Constitutional Law, as well as federal constitutional laws on forming new federation entities in the Russian Federation.

## Article 3. Key Requirements for Acceptance of New Federation Entities into the Russian Federation or Formation of New Federation Entities in the Russian Federation

1.  Acceptance of new federation entities into the Russian Federation or formation of new federation entities in the Russian Federation shall be effected on a voluntary basis.
2.  When accepting new federation entities into the Russian Federation or forming new federation entities in the Russian Federation, the state interests of the Russian Federation, the principles of the federative structure of the Russian Federation, and human and civil rights must be observed; and the existing historical, economic, and cultural ties between Russian Federation entities, as well as their social and economic capacity must be taken into account.

## Article 4. Conditions for Acceptance of New Federation Entities into the Russian Federation

1.  A foreign state or a part thereof may be accepted into the Russian Federation as a new federation entity.
2.  Acceptance of a foreign state or a part thereof into the Russian Federation as a new federation entity shall be effected on mutual consent between the Russian Federation and a given foreign state in consistence with an international (interstate) treaty on accepting a given foreign state or a part thereof into the Russian federation as a new federation entity (hereinafter, an international treaty), concluded between the Russian Federation and a given foreign state.
3.  If a foreign state is accepted into the Russian Federation as a new federation entity, such an entity is accorded the status of a republic, if the international treaty, indicated in Item 2 of this Article, does not envision that the new entity should be accorded the status of a territory or oblast.
4.  If a part of a foreign state is accepted into the Russian Federation as a new federation entity, such an entity is accorded the status of a republic, territory, oblast or autonomous district in consistence with the international treaty, indicated in Item 2 of this Article.

### Article 5. Conditions for the Formation of New Federation Entities in the Russian Federation

1. A new federation entity in the Russian Federation may be formed by amalgamating two or more Russian Federation entities with mutual borders.
2. Formation of a new federation entity in the Russian Federation may involve cancellation of the Russian Federation entities, the territories of which are subject to amalgamation.
3. A change in the name of a Russian Federation entity, envisioned by Part 2, Article 137 of the Constitution of the Russian Federation, shall not entail formation of a new entity in the Russian Federation. The new name of a given Russian Federation entity shall be included in Article 65 of the Constitution of the Russian Federation and published in the new edition of its text.

# Chapter II. Procedure for Accepting a New Entity into the Russian Federation

### Article 6. Proposal on Accepting a New Entity into the Russian Federation

1. The proposal on accepting a foreign state or a part thereof into the Russian Federation as a new federation entity and on concluding an international treaty, envisioned by Item 2, Article 4 of this Federal Constitutional Law, must originate from a given foreign state.
2. On reception of the proposal indicated in Item 1 of this Article, the President of the Russian Federation shall notify the Federation Council of the Federal Assembly of the Russian Federation (here inafter, Federation Council), the State Duma of the Federal Assembly of the Russian Federation (hereinafter, State Duma), the Government of the Russian Federation and, if necessary, shall hold appropriate consultations with them.
3. The proposal indicated in Item 1 of this Article shall be considered, and decisions on the conclusion of an international

treaty shall be made in consistence with the Federal Law "On
International Treaties of the Russian Federation."

## Article 7. Issues Regulated by the International Treaty

1.   The international treaty may regulate the following issues:
     a)   name and status of the new Russian Federation entity;
     b)   procedures, by which the foreign state's citizens will
          acquire Russian Federation citizenship and a full
          legal status of Russian Federation citizens;
     c)   succession of the foreign state in respect of its mem-
          bership in international organizations, its property
          assets and liabilities;
     d)   operation of Russian Federation laws on the territory
          of the new Russian Federation entity;
     e)   functioning of state power and local self-government
          bodies on the territory of the new Russian
          Federation entity.
2.   The international treaty may establish a period of transition,
     during which the new federation entity shall be integrated
     into the economic, financial, crediting, and legal systems of
     the Russian Federation, as well as into the system of the state
     power bodies of the Russian Federation.
3.   The Russian Federation and a given foreign state may sign
     special protocols, to be ratified simultaneously with the inter-
     national treaty, on certain issues pertaining to the acceptance
     of a given foreign state or a part thereof into the Russian
     Federation.
4.   After the signing of the international treaty, the President of
     the Russian Federation shall send an inquiry to the
     Constitutional Court of the Russian Federation requesting to
     review the compliance of a given international treaty with the
     Constitution of the Russian Federation.

## Article 8. Submission of the International Treaty and a Draft Federal Constitutional Law on Accepting a New Entity into the Russian Federation to the State Duma for Ratification

1.   If the Constitutional Court of the Russian Federation finds
     that the not yet effective international treaty conforms to the
     Constitution of the Russian Federation, the international

treaty shall be submitted to the State Duma for ratification in keeping with the procedure, envisioned by the Federal Law "On International Treaties of the Russian Federation".

2. A draft federal constitutional law on accepting a new entity into the Russian Federation shall be submitted to the State Duma simultaneously with the international treaty.

3. The draft federal constitutional law on accepting a new entity into the Russian Federation shall contain provisions determining the name, status, and borders of the new federation entity, as well as final and transitional provisions establishing the terms, by which the new federation entity must be integrated into the economic, financial, crediting, and legal systems of the Russian Federation, as well as into the system of the state power bodies of the Russian Federation. The draft federal constitutional law may also contain other provisions, implied by the international treaty and its protocols.

## Article 9. Adoption and validation of the federal constitutional law on accepting a new entity into the Russian Federation. Introduction of changes into the Constitution of the Russian Federation.

1. The federal law on the international treaty ratification shall be passed by both chambers of the Federal Assembly of the Russian Federation in compliance with the procedure, envisioned by Articles 105, 106, and 107 of the Constitution of the Russian Federation.

2. The federal constitutional law on accepting a new entity into the Russian Federation shall be passed by both chambers of the Federal Assembly of the Russian Federation in compliance with the procedure, envisioned by Article 108 of the Constitution of the Russian Federation.

3. The federal constitutional law on accepting a new entity into the Russian Federation shall come into effect not earlier than the date when the international treaty becomes effective for the Russian Federation and for the foreign state.

4. Changes to Part 1, Article 65 of the Constitution of the Russian Federation, determining the composition of the Russian Federation, shall be introduced based on the federal constitutional law on accepting a new entity into the Russian Federation, and shall be published in the next edition of the text of the Constitution of the Russian Federation. proposals

on the functioning of state bodies and organizations

## Chapter III. Procedure for Forming a New Federation entity in the Russian Federation

### Article 10. Proposal on Forming a New Federation entity in the Russian Federation

1.   The proposal on forming a new federation entity in the Russian Federation must originate from those Russian Federation entities, on the territory of which the new Russian Federation entity is to be formed (hereinafter, Russian Federation entities concerned).

2.   The proposal on forming a new federation entity in the Russian Federation is submitted to the President of the Russian Federation. Such a proposal must be substantiated and must indicate the prospective name, status, and borders of the new federation entity, as well as a forecast of social, economic, and other consequences of the formation of a new entity in the Russian Federation. The proposal shall attach the following accompanying materials:

   a)   proposals on the succession of the new federation entity with respect to the property of the Russian Federation entities concerned and its relations with state power bodies of the Russian Federation and other Russian Federation entities;

   b)   proposals on amendments and changes to the federal law on the federal budget for the current year in connection with the formation of a new federation entity in the Russian Federation, or proposals about the draft federal budget for the following year, if the formation of a new federation entity in the Russian Federation does not involve redistribution of budget resources in the current year;

   c)   proposals on the functioning of state bodies and organizations of the Russian Federation entities concerned on the territory of the new Russian Federation entity, as well as proposals on the formation of state power bodies in the new Russian Federation entity;

   d)   proposals on the operation of the laws and other regulatory acts of the Russian Federation entities concerned on the territory of the new Russian Federation entity; and

e) information on the prospective terms for holding referendums in the Russian Federation entities concerned to vote for the formation of a new entity in the Russian Federation.

3. The President of the Russian Federation shall notify the Council of the Federation, the State Duma, and the Government of the Russian Federation of the proposal to form a new entity in the Russian Federation and, if necessary, shall hold appropriate consultations with them.

## Article 11. Referendums on the Formation of a New Federation Entity in the Russian Federation

1. The issue of forming a new federation entity in the Russian Federation shall be submitted to referendums in the Russian Federation entities concerned.

2. Referendums on forming a new federation entity in the Russian Federation shall be called, prepared and held in the Russian Federation entities concerned in keeping with the laws on referendums of the Russian Federation entities concerned.

3. If the issue of forming a new federation entity in the Russian Federation has been submitted to referendums in two or more Russian Federation entities concerned and has not been supported in at least one of those Russian Federation entities, referendums may be repeated in all Russian Federation entities concerned, regardless of the results of the previous referendums on that issue, not earlier, than after a period of one year.

4. Official data on the results of referendums in the Russian Federation entities concerned on the issue of forming a new federation entity in the Russian Federation shall be submitted to the President of the Russian Federation.

## Article 12. A Draft Federal Constitutional Law on Forming a New Entity in the Russian Federation

1. A draft federal constitutional law on forming a new entity in the Russian Federation may be submitted to the State Duma, if the referendums in the Russian Federation entities concerned have made appropriate decisions on the issue of forming a new federation entity in the Russian Federation. The said draft law shall be submitted by the President of the Russian Federation.

2. A draft federal constitutional law on forming a new entity in the Russian Federation must contain: provisions determining the name, status, and borders of the new Russian Federation entity; provisions on the cancellation of the Russian Federation entity (entities) concerned – in cases, envisioned by Article 5 of this Federal Constitutional Law; as well as final and transitional provisions that establish the terms for regulating the following issues:

    a) forming the state bodies of the new Russian Federation entity;

    b) introducing amendments and changes to the federal law on the federal budget for the current year, if the new federation entity formation involves redistribution of the budget resources for the current year;

    c) succession of the new Russian Federation entity with respect to the property of the Russian Federation entities concerned and its relations with state power bodies of the Russian Federation, other Russian Federation entities, foreign states and international organizations;

    d) functioning of territorial federal bodies and federal courts on the territory of the new Russian Federation entity;

    e) functioning of state bodies and organizations of the Russian Federation entities concerned on the territory of the new Russian Federation entity;

    f) operation of laws and other regulatory acts of the Russian Federation entities concerned on the territory of the new Russian Federation entity

**Article 13. Adoption of a Federal Constitutional Law on the Formation of a New Entity in the Russian Federation. Introduction of Changes to the Constitution of the Russian Federation**

1. A federal constitutional law on the formation of a new entity in the Russian Federation shall be adopted by both chambers of the Federal Assembly of the Russian Federation in keeping with the procedure, envisioned by Article 108 of the Constitution of the Russian Federation.

2. Changes to Part 1, Article 65 of the Constitution of the Russian Federation, which determines the composition of the Russian Federation, shall be introduced based on the federal constitutional law on the formation of a new entity in the Russian Federation and published in the next edition of the Constitution of the Russian Federation.

# Chapter IV. Final Provisions

## Article 14. Effective Date of this Federal Constitutional Law

This Federal Constitutional Law shall come into effect as of the date of its official publication.

# Appendix II
# Agreement on Single Economic Space

On April 19, 2004, the leaders of Belarus, Kazakhstan, Russia and Ukraine signed an Agreement to form a Single Economic Space.

## The Agreement on Single Economic Space

The Republic of Belarus, the Republic of Kazakhstan, the Russian Federation and Ukraine, hereby referred to as Parties,
- in pursuit of economic and social progress of the above nations and higher standards of living;
- driven by the desire to strengthen the economies of the Parties and provide for their harmonious development, consistency in economic reformation and further expansion of multilateral economic cooperation, and intensifying the process of integration by achieving mutual ly-beneficial accords to form a Single Economic Space (SES);
- in recognition the right of the Parties to determine their involvement in the formation of the SES depending on their preparedness for further intensification of the integration process;
- reaffirming friendly relations between the governments and the people, with their prosperity in mind, and guided by commonly recognized principles and rules of international law; and
- in consideration of the Joint Statement of the Presidents of the Republic of Belarus, the Republic of Kazakhstan, the Russian Federation and Ukraine made on February 23, 2003;
the Parties hereby agree to the following:

## Article 1

In order to provide for the stable and efficient development of the economies of the Parties and higher living standards of their people, the Parties shall initiate the process of forming the SES.

Single Economic Space is to be understood as an economic dimension combining customs territories of the Parties, where the function of economic regulation is based on common principles of securing a free flow of goods, services, capital and labor force and the pursuit of a single foreign trade policy, while the taxation, lend-ing and monetary policies are coordinated to the extent necessary to assure equitable market competition and to maintain macroeconomic stability.

The Parties shall strive to facilitate
- the development of trade and investment between the Parties provid
  ing for sustainable development of the Parties' economies based on
  the commonly recognized principles and rules of international law,
  and also rules and principles of the WTO;
-the strengthening of the unity and growth of economic potentials,
  and the growth of competitive capacity of the Parties' economies in
  foreign markets.

## Article 2

A phased approach to accomplishing the goal of deeper integration is premised on the fulfillment of the obligations accepted by the Parties and actual completion of the following tasks:
- the establishment of a free-trade area without exceptions and restric-
  tions, with the intention of abstaining from anti-dumping, compensa-
  tory and special protection measures in mutual trade, and based on a
  single policy toward tariff and non-tariff regulation, unified rules for
  market competition, provision of subsidies and other forms of govern
  ment support;
- the unification of the principles of development and application of
  technical regulations and standards, and sanitary and phyto-sanitary
  rules; - the harmonization of macroeconomic policies;
- the providing for a free flow of goods, services, capital, and labor;
- the harmonization of the Parties' laws to the extent necessary for the
  functioning of the SES, including trade and market competition poli
  cies;
-the establishment of unified principles for regulating the operation of
  natural monopolies (railroad transportation, long-distance telecom
  munications, transmission of power, oil and gas, and in other sec
  tors), unified market competition rules and the enforcement of non-
  discriminatory access and rates for services provided by natural
  monopolies.

## Article 3

In accordance with the goals and tasks stated in Article 1 and 2 of this Agreement,the Parties will take actions, stipulated in the Single Economic Space Concept which shall be attached as an integral part of this Agreement.
For the implementation of this Agreement, the Parties shall develop the Principal Action Plan Package for the formation of the Single Economic Space.

## Article 4

The processes of the establishment and operation of the SES shall be coordinated by appropriate bodies, which shall be structured to accommodate the extent of the integration.

SES bodies shall be established by combining an intergovernmental component with the principle that the Parties shall delegate some of their authorities to a single regulatory body, whose prominence shall increase gradually.

At the inter-governmental level, the coordination and control over the formation and operation of the SES shall be provided by the Council of the Heads of States (CHS).

The voting for all member countries within the CHS is based on the principle "one country – one vote." The CHS shall rule by consensus.

The Parties shall institute a single regulatory body for the SES and, in accordance with the international agreements, they will delegate some of their authority to it. Its decisions shall be mandatory for compliance by every Party.

The single regulatory body of the SES shall rule on all issues by weighted voting. The number of votes for each Party is premised on its economic potential. The vote assignment shall be based on the agreement between the Parties.

All the Parties have the right to appeal the ruling of the single regulatory body of the SES to the CHS.

A separate international agreement shall provide for a mechanism of compensation in the event when a ruling causes substantial economic loss to one or more Parties.

## Article 5

The SES shall be phased in with the possibility [for the Parties] to differ in the level of the involvement and the pace of the integration.

Transition from one phase to the next one shall be taken by the Parties who shall have undertaken to the full extent all the actions assigned to the former phase by the Principal Action Plan Package for the formation of the Single Economic Space.

The Parties shall accede to the international Agreements on the formation and operation of the SES as they complete their preparations. All Parties shall observe an agreed sequential procedure of accession to these Agreements. No Party shall hinder other Parties' accelerated progress toward higher degree of integration.

The difference in the level of the involvement and the pace of the integration essentially means that each Party shall independently decide which areas of integration and which integrated facilities it would get involved in and to what extent.

## Article 6

The legal basis for the formation and operation of the SES shall be laid down by the international Agreements; the rulings of the SES bodies shall comply with the laws of the Parties and the commonly recognized rules and principles of international law.

## Article 7

Disputes and disagreements between the Parties concerning the interpretation and/or practical application of this Agreement shall be resolved through consultations and negotiations.

## Article 8

This Agreement is open for the accession by other nations who share its goals and principles on the terms agreed on by all the Parties to this Agreement.

For an acceding country, this Agreement takes effect on the date when the depository receives the last notice of consent to the accession addressed to the Parties.

## Article 9

By mutual consent of Parties, this Agreement can be amended and expanded through separate protocols, which shall become an integral part of this Agreement and take effect as stipulated in Article 10 of this Agreement.

## Article 10

This Agreement shall take effect on the date when the depository receives the last written notice on the completion of the domestic government procedures necessary for the Agreement to take effect.

# About the Author

In 1982, Herman Pirchner, Jr. became the founding President of the American Foreign Policy Council (AFPC), a non-profit public policy organization headquartered in Washington, DC. Under his leadership, AFPC has become widely recognized as an important source of timely, insightful analysis on issues of foreign policy. It works closely with Members of Congress, the Executive Branch and the policymaking community, and serves as a valuable resource to officials in the highest levels of government. AFPC regularly hosts the Washington visits of high-level foreign dignitaries, conducts briefings for Members of Congress and their staffs on critical foreign policy issues, and leads fact-finding missions abroad for current and former American officials. A noted expert on Russian foreign and domestic policy, Mr. Pirchner has visited the Russian Federation 54 times since 1989.

www.ingramcontent.com/pod-product-compliance
Lightning Source LLC
Chambersburg PA
CBHW021824270326
41932CB00007B/321